DELTA TEACHER DEVELOPMENT SERIES

Series editors Mike Burghall and Lindsay Clandfield

Storytelling With Our Students

Techniques for telling tales from around the world

David Heathfield

Published by
DELTA PUBLISHING
Quince Cottage
Hoe Lane
Peaslake
Surrey GU5 9SW
England

www.deltapublishing.co.uk

© Delta Publishing 2014

ISBN 978-1-905085-87-3

Edited by Mike Burghall
Designed by Christine Cox
Cover photo © TomaB/Shutterstock.com
Illustration © stdemi/iStockphoto.com
Printed in Greece by Bakis AEBE

Dedication

This book is dedicated to my sons Tom and Sam.

Acknowledgements

I send my heartfelt thanks to:

All the storytellers who have freely given me their stories.

My parents Raymond and Beryl Heathfield, who told Jan, Kathy, Alison and me stories when we were very young.

Peter Hamilton, whose inspirational theatre-making taught me about storytelling.

Geoff Fox, who showed me how to do storytelling in the first place and who continues to give me guidance.

Mario Rinvolucri, who introduced me to the power of storytelling in language teaching and who was the first person to tell me I was a storyteller.

Andrew Wright, who has inspired me and countless other teachers and students across the world to tell stories.

Nick Bilbrough, who shares great passion for the storytelling courses we offer teachers.

Mike Burghall, the editor of *Storytelling With Our Students*, who has drawn all of these ideas out of me and made sense of them; and Christine Cox, who has designed this book with such talent and patience.

Tammy Heathfield, who gives her love and support to me as I make my way through life as a storyteller.

Students and teachers and all others who share the joys of storytelling with me.

You, a teller of stories.

From the author

'A journey of a thousand miles must begin with a single step.'
Laozi
Chinese philosopher, 6th century BC

About twenty years ago, I joined a storytelling workshop led by Dr Geoff Fox, a fellow member of The Brown Paper Bag Theatre Company in Crediton, Devon, UK. The plan was for members of the cast to prepare well-known Robin Hood stories to tell students in Exeter schools on the day before we actually performed our play, *Robin Hood to the Rescue*, in the school grounds in the evening.

Although I had experience of theatre acting, this was to be my first attempt at classroom storytelling without a script. Geoff is an experienced storyteller and an excellent teacher, and in his workshop he had us all putting away the *printed* word and telling our stories in our *own* words.

What had seemed like a huge step was in fact a simple 'letting go'.

The stories sprang to life, and we quickly discovered that – each time one of us told our story – the way we told it became more and more our own. We didn't just find our own *words* to tell the story, we were telling the story using our imaginations, bodies, faces and voices – until the stories were no longer coming from the book but from our 'selves'.

I arrived at the first school, brimming with confidence.

But storytelling at that school was challenging for me. I had never met the students before, and the teacher had left them alone with me. I waited and waited for the teacher to arrive and introduce me, while the students became more and more over-excited. What was she thinking of? She still didn't turn up, so I threw myself into the storytelling – and just about managed to keep the attention of a classroom full of lively young people.

It was the first time I had told a story in a classroom, and it wasn't even with my own students. Those students had never had a storyteller come into their class before. No wonder the energy was high!

Looking back, Geoff is amazed that I went on to become a storyteller after that baptism of fire.

Following that experience, I ran an end-of-day workshop on storytelling for a couple of colleagues in the language school where I was joint Director of Studies, and began experimenting with classroom storytelling. What I saw initially as an add-on skill quickly developed into a core aspect of my teaching.

Teacher – and student – storytelling and drama are the most effective ways I know of students developing their listening and speaking skills, critical thinking skills and creativity.

In 2004 I reduced my classroom teaching hours, and have worked as a freelance storyteller on a part-time basis alongside my teaching ever since. I tell stories with adults, teenagers and children of all ages from three years up.

Many people I work with are learning English in the UK, where I live, or in other parts of the world. Many others are English speakers who want to learn about different cultures through their traditional stories.

I'm very fortunate to run storytelling workshops with teachers working around the world. In this way, I have become fascinated by intercultural storytelling, and have learned many stories by listening to them being told by students and teachers from everywhere. You will notice this as you discover the stories I have retold in this book.

Storytelling to celebrate diversity has also led me to learn about multi-sensory storytelling with people who have learning difficulties, with people who have sensory impairments and people with other kinds of physical or mental difference.

Rhythm, sound, movement and touch enhance the storytelling I do: not only for those with special needs, but for *everyone*. Storytelling engages the whole person – mind, body and emotions – and these are inseparable from language and communication.

Opening this book may be your first step, or perhaps your storytelling journey is already well under way …

David

david@davidheathfield.co.uk
www.davidheathfield.co.uk

Contents

From the author — Page 3

Part A — Page 7

Telling techniques for telling tales — Page 25

Part B — Page 37

Chapter One
The teacher as storyteller — Page 39

Using your voice — Page 40
The Story of Sidwell

Giving the characters voices — Page 42
The Dog and the Wolf

Facial expression — Page 44
The Village of Fools

Movement and gesture — Page 45
Ngaardi and Toonkoo

Mimed actions — Page 46
Manju

Accompanying the story — Page 48
Filling the House

Repetition of words — Page 50
Maui and the Great Fish

Repetition of phrases — Page 52
Anansi and Tiger

Repetition of phrases with alterations — Page 54
Lazy Jack

Repetition of rhymes — Page 56
Juan and the Magic Tree

Repetition of episodes — Page 58
The Witch of Tavistock

Interacting with the characters — Page 60
Bedd Gelert

Interacting with the students — Page 62
How to Weigh an Elephant

Interacting through interruptions — Page 63
Cloud Eating

Interacting through riddles — Page 64
A Question of Brains

Interacting through different cultures — Page 66
The Three Golden Hairs
Jackal and the Shining Child

Interacting through personalisation — Page 68
The Lost Axe

Chapter Two — Page 69
Creative ways into and out of storytelling

From story to lesson — Page 70
The Teacher

Predicting the story — Page 71
Little Dog, Panther and Monkey

Asking and imagining — Page 72
The Small Bird's Wisdom

Imagining and improvising — Page 74
Aldar Kose Tricks the Bai

Contents

Freeze!   Page 76
Dongguo and the Wolf

Act it out!   Page 78
The Coat

Responding in role   Page 80
Garuda and Turtle

Responding with a task   Page 82
The Snowgirl

Reponding with a gift   Page 84
Mbongoro

Responding personally   Page 86
The Fly

Exploring metaphor   Page 88
The Snake Wife

Exploring mental imagery   Page 90
After the Fire

Exploring meaning   Page 92
The Ferryman and the Grammar Teacher

Chapter Three   Page 93
The student as storyteller

From repeating to retelling   Page 94
Li and Gao

From miming to retelling   Page 95
The Sleeve

Mapping a story   Page 96
The Bridge

Stepping through a story   Page 98
The Silver in the Fireplace

Retelling a story in character   Page 100
How Spider Got a Narrow Waist

Retelling a story in images   Page 102
Sand and Stone

Creating a new ending   Page 104
The Talking Skull

Performing a new ending   Page 106
The Snake and the King's Dreams

From storytelling to storymaking   Page 108
The Seven Parrots

Part C   Page 111

In the classroom   Page 111

Beyond the classroom   Page 117

Joining forces   Page 119

Courses   Page 120

Sources   Page 122

From the editors   Page 127

From the publisher   Page 128

Anansi the Spider wanted all the wisdom in the world just for himself, and he knew the wisdom was in the sky god's stories.

Using all his tricks, greedy Anansi got hold of all the stories, closed them in a box and tied it to his belly.
'I'll climb the tallest tree and hide my box of stories at the top where no one else can ever find them.'

Anansi started climbing up the tree, but the box tied to his belly kept knocking against the trunk of the tree.

He climbed higher and higher, but the box was bothering him more and more.

Then Anansi heard the sound of a child laughing at him from the bottom of the tree.

'Are you laughing at me?'
'Yes,' cried the child 'because you're a fool, Anansi!'
'You're wrong!' shouted Anansi, 'I have all the wisdom. All the stories in the world are in my box!'

The child laughed still louder.
'Then why are you carrying the box tied to your belly, so it knocks against the tree trunk? You should have it tied to your back!'

Anansi knew the child was speaking the truth. In his anger, he untied the box and threw it down at the child.

The box went flying down towards the child, but it struck a branch of the tree. The box broke open and all of the stories came out.

The stories were carried away on the breeze, floating across the oceans and the forests and the mountains of the whole world.

Slowly the stories drifted down and landed on every one of us.

That's why we all carry stories with us.

We are all storytellers.

A West African folk tale

Storytelling with our students

We are all storytellers. We humans make sense of the world around us through stories.

We spend much of our waking time in daydream moments: retelling to ourselves what happened, what we wish had happened, imagining what is likely to happen in the future and what we fantasise might happen.

We filter everything going on around us, and turn what we select into stories.

The word 'storytelling' is used in a multitude of contexts related to day-to-day conversation, the media, the arts, faith, business and therapy – wherever narratives play a central role:

- Anecdotes, and even pieces of gossip, are the stories that make up everyday conversation.
- Reporters try to make sense of world events by telling news stories.
- Film directors use sound and vision, as well as words, to tell stories.
- Choreographers tell stories through movement.
- Religion and story are inseparable; the faithful learn how they should act, through the stories told by prophets and through the stories of the prophets' own lives.
- Every business has a shared story, everyone working in that business has their own employment narrative, and every transaction is a story in itself.
- Personal storytelling seems to be the most effective healing process whenever we suffer psychological hurt.

Storytelling is what sets us apart from other creatures living on this planet, and goes back to the beginnings of humankind – when we needed to share wisdom in our communities, about real and imagined experiences and about our dreams, fears and wishes.

Storytelling With Our Students is about the satisfaction and learning the people we teach derive from being told, and telling, tales from the world's oral cultures.

Storytelling across time

Storytelling began at the dawn of human culture, and the power of the earliest tales we have on record – such as the Sumerian *Epic of Gilgamesh*, which was carved on stone tablets in Mesopotamia four thousand years ago – resonates down through the ages.

Since ancient times, rhythm, vocalisation, gesture, mime, dance, objects and pictures have all been at the heart of storytelling, alongside verbal language. Little has changed, when it comes to traditional storytelling, since its earliest origins.

The work of Dr Alida Gersie with storytelling in the fields of therapy and education provides

After nourishment, shelter and companionship, stories are the thing we need most in the world.

Philip Pullman

7

insight into the potential storytelling offers us:

'Stories alert us to the possibilities of betterment. Not necessarily because they have happy endings. Old folktales don't. But because the story evokes in the listener an 'if only' response, jolting us into the awareness that life could be different, both for better and for worse. We are reminded of alternatives. Our attention is directed towards the unexplained and the unexpected. In stories a known situation functions as the starting point for an exploration of the not-yet-known, that which surprises and maybe frightens us. Through listening to the ancient tales we are offered increased knowledge of various ways to approach the unfamiliar. What we do with this knowledge is for us to decide.' [1]

Traditional storytelling generally refers to the folk tales and myths which are shared by members of a community, and which have been passed down by word of mouth from generation to generation over tens, hundreds or thousands of years – so that it can be difficult to trace their origins.

This is the kind of storytelling we are dealing with in this book.

Storytelling in modern times

Neuroscientist Antonio Damasio points out: *'The problem of how to make … wisdom understandable, transmissible, persuasive, enforceable – in a word, of how to make it stick – was faced and a solution was found. Storytelling was the solution – storytelling is something brains do, naturally and implicitly … [It] should be no surprise that it pervades the entire fabric of human societies and cultures.'* [2]

- Sadly, there are millions of people today who have never experienced the joy of being told a folk tale or of retelling one. This is a new phenomenon: it would be unimaginable for our ancestors to live in a world without this kind of oral storytelling. For tens of thousands of years, 'homo sapiens' has been telling and listening to folk tales but, recently, some of us have lost the habit.
- The good news, however, is that people are becoming aware, once again, of the power and value of storytelling. Recent research in the fields of neuroscience, psychology and education tells us what we already know: *'Our brain is hardwired to respond to story.'* [3]

Just notice how people respond when they are engaged in listening to a well-told folk tale. They 'live' through the story, identifying closely with the struggles of the protagonist. Experimental psychologist Stephen Pinker writes: *'A recent brain-imaging study reported in Psychological Science reveals that the regions of the brain that process the sights, sounds, tastes and movement of real life are activated when we are engrossed in a compelling narrative.'* [4]

Storytelling across the world

Many have analysed what a folk tale is, since Vladimir Propp published *The Morphology of the Folktale* in 1927 [5] and identified certain central motifs:

- A folk tale involves the protagonist becoming absent from the protecting authority of the world he or she knows. For example, the mother dies or the hero runs away or is sent away.
- A folk tale takes the listener through highs and lows, as the events are told one after the other in sequence. For example, the protagonist is abducted then liberated, then ignores warnings from the liberator and faces mortal danger from the abductor, then overcomes the abductor and finally finds fulfilment with the help of the liberator.
- The functions of the characters are constant elements. For example, the central protagonist or hero undergoes a test, or the hero is given something magical – it is the act of testing or giving that is more central to folk tales than whether it is a brother or a wise woman or a king who does the testing or gives the magical gift.
- There is often a multiplication (a duplicating, tripling or quadrupling) of a function in a folk tale. For example, many European tales feature a third heroic sibling – who completes a task after the two older siblings have failed – or a protagonist undergoes three tests.

As a story is passed down through time, the overall plot, core message and inherent learning remain largely unchanged, although characters, symbols and settings may alter, especially as

The Universe began as story.

Ben Okri

It is the people who die off, not the tales.

Jakob and Wilhelm Grimm

stories spread to different regions. Tortoise is the trickster in some parts of West Africa, while Rabbit is the trickster in others – but many of the stories told about both of these characters are essentially the same.

Details in the story change from one storyteller to the next, so that every storyteller puts their own unique stamp on the story. Listeners know intuitively what needs to remain and what they can adapt when *they* become the storytellers and pass on the stories to members of *their* families and communities and, indeed, to people from other communities.

Every culture around the world has its own storytelling tradition and, in some cultures, this oral transmission of stories continues uninterrupted today. However, with the arrival of written literacy, there has been a trend over the last couple of centuries for the reading of published stories to replace oral storytelling.

- An extremely positive result of this is that millions of traditional folk tales from cultures around the world have been published in anthologies and, more recently, online.
- And many of us have had folk tales read to us from books such as *Grimm's Fairy Tales*.

Storytelling in the community

As storyteller Andrew Wright explains: '*Each culture offers stories representing its own values and perceptions and behaviour and these can help individuals and societies to establish their sense of identity.*' [6]

Whereas reading and writing stories tend to be solitary activities, story 'telling' is fundamentally an interpersonal activity, and this builds relationships and community. Knowing the stories of our own communities helps bind us together, giving us a sense of belonging. Traditionally, folk tales are told and retold – and this is part of their power.

Every time the story is told, it is created anew. According to Bob Barton and David Booth: '*We see that story from our own perspectives, using our experiences to make new sense of that story ... [Storytelling] is a co-creative or re-creative act. As we retell a story, we resynthesise and restate ourselves, in our present versions.*' [7]

Today, we live in a globalising world where there is an ever-increasing need for us to learn from cultures beyond our own.

Nasrudin Hodja is the Turkish name for the 'wise fool' who appears in short tales told across Asia, North Africa, Central Europe and the Balkans – a few of them are in this book. Other names for him include Joha (see page 21), Mullah, Effendi and Dheju. The wisdom and humour in these tales are inextricably linked – as in the one below, which illustrates the usually unfounded fear of the unknown 'other'. (You can listen to me telling it with learners of English by going to *www.youtube.com* and then searching for David Heathfield Why are we here?)

Why are we here?

Nasrudin Hodja walked along the road, leaving his own land for the first time. He wondered how people would treat him in this new land.

Coming towards him, Nasrudin saw three men on horseback. Would they greet him? Would they ignore him? Would they attack him? He became so afraid that he ran and climbed over the nearest wall and found himself in a graveyard. He hid in a freshly-dug grave, trembling with fear.

Seeing the stranger's unusual behaviour, the three horsemen were curious. They stopped and climbed over the same wall and looked for him in the graveyard. They stood looking down and smiling at the trembling stranger in the grave: 'Please forgive us for asking, but why are you here?'

Nasrudin looked up at the three kind faces: 'That is a difficult question to answer. I am here because of you, and you are here because of me.'

Storytelling and teaching

Storytelling – the art of telling an unscripted story directly to listeners – is the most widely-used and long-established way of transferring information and, as applied linguist Ruth Wajnryb explains: *'[it] is as old as time, and certainly predates the construction of the very modern notion of classroom … with the capacity to transport the hearer beyond all boundaries of time, space, language, ethnicity, class and gender.'* [8]

The classes we teach are also communities, and it is our role as teachers to do all we can to ensure that the community's needs are met. Sharing stories plays a key role. While listening to *us* telling folk tales and myths, and then retelling them in *their* own words, students are interpreting meanings relevant to their own life experiences.

Interpretation

These interpretations are both collective and highly individual.
- The story *The Hare and the Tortoise* inevitably makes English-speaking listeners think of the English saying 'Slow and steady wins the race'.
- Speakers of other languages think of equivalent sayings.

However, the way individual listeners relate the story to their own lives depends on factors such as their personal values, their current concerns, their beliefs and perceptions about themselves in relation to others, their mood and their state of health and well-being.

The archetypal characters who feature in folk tales remind listeners of people they know. For me, Hare's actions bring to mind an ex-colleague who used to stand in the middle of the staffroom every breaktime and boast, listing her achievements at the top of her voice.

These archetypes also represent aspects of the listeners' own selves.
- At the moment of writing this paragraph, I feel like Tortoise. I am the slowest writer I know, and every phrase requires time and effort. My mantra today is 'Slow and steady wins the race'. In fact, I wish I had a little of Hare's apparent self-assurance and bravado.
- But tomorrow morning at nine o'clock, I'll be telling Grimm's fairy tales to 200 children at a primary school assembly and, if I'm not careful, I'll be as full of myself as Hare at the start of the race!

In the words of Barton and Booth: *'Story causes us to tap into the universal situations of life, to stand in the shoes of others in all the world's past, present and future, taking risks, suffering, sorrowing, laughing, wondering, challenging, feeling satisfied but, most of all, tuning into the archetypes of all story wisdom.'* [9]

The storytelling techniques and activities in *Storytelling With Our Students* make it possible for our students to develop their creativity, their critical thinking skills and self-expression, and to become more aware of their own perspectives and those of their fellow students.

A co-creative process

Every time you find the way to convey a story to your students, you are re-creating the story anew, and this spontaneous creative act is mirrored in the co-creating of the story in your students' imaginations.

There is now evidence of 'neural coupling' between speaker and listener during storytelling: in other words, the listener's brain activity mirrors the storyteller's activity. An experiment reported in 2010 states: *'We connected the extent of neural coupling to a quantitative measure of story comprehension and find that the greater the anticipatory speaker–listener coupling, the greater the understanding.'* [10]
- The listener's brain is as active as the storyteller's and is, in fact, telling and anticipating the story *internally* along with you.
- You can also give your students the opportunity to tell the story *externally* along with you, both verbally and physically, and even influence the course the story takes.

This level of interaction has a positive effect on the class as a learning community and, when students know they can – as class members – influence the way a story develops, they will become more aware of their own creative potential as storytellers.

Cultural diversity

As Ruth Wajnryb puts it: *'The primacy and enduring quality of storytelling are no doubt linked to its role through time in the maintenance of ethnic culture – essentially the way in which a collective group of people maintains and bequeaths its sense of its own identity.'* [11]

- Teachers can bring stories from all oral cultures to life in their teaching, whether their classes are mono-cultural or ethnically diverse, and not only from those cultures represented in the classroom.
- Students in all multi-cultural and mono-cultural classes benefit from opportunities to step into the imaginative landscapes of other cultures, and storytelling is an ideal medium for this.

There have been great societies that did not use the wheel, but there have been no societies that did not tell stories.

Ursula K. Le Guin

A traditional folk tale from a particular culture often has both universal motifs and culturally specific details.

- The universality makes the story more accessible to students from a different culture.
- At the same time, culturally specific details offer them an insight into what makes that culture unique.

The folk tales in this book come from cultures all around the world – to reflect this wonderful 'world of stories' we inhabit.

For example, the Japanese folk tale *Manju* (see page 47) features Mr Pine, an archetypal trickster. Similar trickster characters appear in tales from every region of the world – Maui from New Zealand (page 51), Anansi from the Caribbean and West Africa (page 6 and page 52), Jackal from Southern Africa (page 67), Little Dog from Venezuela (page 71), the Small Bird from Poland (page 73), Aldar Kose from Kazakstan (page 75), Turtle from Thailand (page 81). They are instantly recognisable as tricksters, even though they manifest themselves as different kinds of animals, humans and deities in different cultures.

However culturally specific you are, the humour that really works, it works because it's funny and touches something we all recognize.

Meera Syal

Here are just three examples of culturally specific features:

- In the *Manju* tale, one of the friends believes that foxes turn into ghosts. This is a recurring motif in Japanese folklore.
- In *Maui and the Great Fish*, Maui, the youngest brother, is a deity who has the strength to pull New Zealand up from under the sea. This gives us insight into traditional Maori beliefs which are valued and still celebrated by modern New Zealanders.
- *Anansi and Tiger* features the demi-god Anansi, the half-man half-spider at the centre of the web of Caribbean and West African folklore.

Cultural diversity can easily be celebrated through the sharing of stories, and this kind of intercultural storytelling leads to bridging cultures. In a class where there is at least one student from a minority ethnic group, one way of raising awareness of that student's heritage is through storytelling.

Cultural understanding

Students may be able to bring in a story from their own culture to tell in class but, even before this happens, teachers can play a key role in enabling that student's cultural background to be celebrated. Resources like this book make it easier to find folk tales from all cultures, written down in English.

I was invited by the Anglo-Polish Organisation in mid-Devon to do a project telling popular Polish folk tales and doing follow-up workshops in several local schools where there was a small minority of students who had recently arrived to live long-term in the UK from Poland with their parents.

- The students were facing challenges integrating into their new communities. Telling the tales that the Polish students already knew led to the local British-born students

acknowledging, esteeming and wanting to know more about their Polish classmates' culture and language.
- Their teachers commented on the confidence that the project gave the Polish students to express themselves, and it gave the students a break from putting all their energy into fitting into the dominant culture.

The result was that genuine deep intercultural sharing took place in the process. The most popular tale of all was *Jaś and Małgosia*, a Polish variant of 'Hansel and Gretel', featuring the terrifying Baba Yaga. *'Between different cultures there are common features and themes evident in many traditional folk tales. When exchanging stories in this way, both the commonalities and the cultural differences give rise to mutual understanding.'* [12] (There is a video of me telling the story at *www.youtube.com* – search for David Heathfield Jas and Malgosia.)

And thereby hangs a tale.

William Shakespeare

On one occasion, I was hosting an intimate evening event designed to raise awareness of the cultures represented by newly-arrived international students at the University of Exeter. Several students sang songs and recited poems. Among the Asian, Middle-Eastern and European students was one African student, a Nigerian woman called Ifeoma Nwokolo starting her foundation year. Although there was a convivial atmosphere, she was reluctant to perform, despite encouragement from her peers.
- During the break, I sought her permission to tell a Nigerian story from the Igbo culture, Ifeoma's own ethnic group. I made it clear to the audience that I was representing Ifeoma when I told the story.
- Six months later, she made a point of thanking me for including her and her culture on that evening. She had felt acknowledged in her new international community at the university and said 'it made me feel at home'.

Of course, the telling of a story in English from a culture *other* than that of the teacher and their students also promotes intercultural understanding. For example, when students are studying material about some aspect of another country such as New Zealand or Turkey, why not tell a traditional Maori or Turkish tale in order to awaken their curiosity and awareness of those cultures?

Storytelling and the teacher

There are few joys to compare with the telling of a well-told tale.

Charles de Lint

There is an important difference which, as 'storytelling teachers', we should be aware of – the difference between *telling* a story and *reading* a story to our students.
- Reading novels and poems aloud from the page makes sense because the text has been carefully crafted by a single *writer*.
- Oral stories – in other words, folk tales, fables, myths, legends and fairy stories – come from the *oral* tradition and have been created and re-created and honed by generations of tellers and listeners, and so they are best told without referring to a written text.

Transmitting a tale

A story you are told is one storyteller's version of that ever-evolving story as it reaches your ears. If you choose to re-create that story by passing it on, you spend time getting to the heart of the story, finding your own way of retelling it and then rehearsing it. And each time you retell the story, you are re-creating it for yourself, as well as for your students.

'If a teacher reads the story from a book the page is often between her and the students. When she tells, she is a fountain and the words of the story gush forth from her. She and the story are one as the water is with the fountain.' [13]

Another important difference is that, when you tell a story, there is no book, photocopy or screen 'in the way'. Your students will sense immediately that you are telling the story in your own words – that the story is a gift, from you to them.
- Some teachers initially doubt their ability to tell a story but, in my experience, teachers nearly always have a hidden talent for storytelling.

- In fact, teachers are nearly always much better at telling stories than they are at reading them aloud.

The versions of the folk tales that appear in *Storytelling With Our Students* are adapted from transcriptions of me telling the stories with *my* students. (You can see or hear them all on YouTube – see page 36 for more details.)

However, I urge you to find *your own way* of telling these or other stories. You might follow some of the advice offered in 'Preparing to tell a tale' below.

- For those of you who are new to storytelling in your classes, here is an opportunity to add a new dimension to your teaching.
- For those experienced classroom storytellers, this book may act as a reminder of why storytelling is so vital to intercultural and interpersonal communication and, I hope, there are plenty of new ideas for you to learn from.

Selecting a tale to tell

Folk tales I tell are often ones I've learnt by listening, not only to my students, but also to teachers and other storytellers I have met. I often ask people to tell me a short folk tale and, if I know that I want to tell it myself, I ask them permission to pass it on.

- Usually I have my mp3 player or mobile to hand, and I immediately record myself telling the story back to the person who gave it to me so I can remember it.
- I ask them to interrupt me if I make a mistake or miss something out.

I learn still more stories by reading in anthologies of folk tales and, increasingly, I find these for free on the Web.

So when there are so many folk tales available, how do you select your tales and then prepare to 'tell' them?

It is important that you enjoy and are able to feel your way into the tale when you first come across it – that you know that it's a story you'd like to tell, and you can imagine your students doing one or more of the following: being engaged, discovering truth in their own way, developing empathy, being imaginative and appreciating difference. [14]

Of course, taking into account the age of the students you're working with is essential:

- In children's folk tales, wishes are typically fulfilled and the protagonist returns to a safe place.
- However, in folk tales which are appropriate for young adults, this wish-fulfillment accompanies the protagonist taking on the role of the parent so that the higher authority is no longer troublesome. These are the stories of someone struggling with what it means to be without a parent figure, what it means to live with strangers. Is it possible to make a life where you don't fit? This is not an unusual question for young adults. [15]

Life itself is the most wonderful fairytale of all.

Hans Christian Andersen

The folk tales I have chosen for *Storytelling With Our Students* are all short tales which are suitable for telling with people aged from eight to one hundred years old – I recently told stories at a remarkable old lady's one hundredth birthday celebration in a care home. Many of the tales I tell are much longer, but most often in our classes it makes sense to tell tales which are short, simple and powerful.

Building a repertoire of tales

It is advisable to let your storytelling repertoire evolve slowly.

- Try out the same story with different classes if you can.
- You'll probably find that each class responds very differently, and so your telling will vary as well.

If you've heard this story before, don't stop me, because I'd like to hear it again.

Groucho Marx

It makes sense to learn one story and tell it five times, rather than learn five stories and tell each of them once.

- You could use the folk tales in this book as starting points, but do remember that they have been selected by *me* because they suit *me* as a storyteller – although I do believe *your* students might enjoy being told these stories.

- However, *you* need to want to tell the stories *you* choose, so it's a good idea to find and tell some of your own favourites too. (Useful sources are listed on page 122.)

But if you feel the story you've just told wasn't the right one for your students, don't discard it too soon. It might be just the right story for another class at another moment.

In the words of my teacher training colleague Nick Bilbrough: '*As any experienced teacher and any experienced learner knows, the human factor is what makes the classroom a unique place: the fact that different people, at different times, will respond to activities in different ways. An activity is defined through its interaction with the learners.*' [16]

Preparing to tell a tale

After you have been told or have read a story for the first time, you are likely to remember a few strong mental images and some key words and phrases.

- You could jot down a skeleton version of the story, or map the story as a series of quick sketches – dividing it into short and simple episodes.
- You could then read the story again – or ask for it to be told again, if possible – and add any key moments to your skeleton or map.

The sooner you start practising telling the story in your own words without reference to the source, whether to a family member, a friend, a colleague or to yourself (perhaps video-recording yourself on your mobile phone), the sooner you'll find your own way of telling it.

- You might then go back to the source a final time to check, but don't let that version have too much influence on your own telling of the tale.
- You might then rehearse with a simple prop or a percussive or musical instrument, if you feel this will enhance your telling of the story.

Varying the volume, pitch and tempo of your voice will draw listeners in.

- It's a good idea to use plenty of direct speech in most kinds of folk tale, so you can play with the characters' voices and mannerisms.
- It's a good idea, often, to make up a phrase or rhyme, accompanied by a mime, which the students can join in with.

The important thing is not to overdo any of these things. Hinting at something with a subtle action is usually more effective than a huge, exaggerated gesture. You don't want to break the spell of the storytelling experience.

Finally, practise the beginning and the ending again:

- You want to make an impact and signal clearly to your students that the story has begun and has ended.
- What happens between can be much more flexible and responsive.

Before you tell a tale

You might ask yourself these questions:

- How am I going to link this story to the rest of the course? Or the lesson?
- How am I going to lead into the story, and how am I going to follow it up?

And these:

- Which is the best place to tell the story? Is there a more suitable space than the classroom?
- How shall I arrange the space? Is it possible to move the tables aside and have no physical barriers between me and the students?
- Would it work better for my students to be sitting on the floor or on chairs?
- If we can't move the desks, could I ask the students to put their things away so that they don't get distracted?
- Where am I going to sit or stand? How much space do I need between me and the students?
- Can I create an intimate atmosphere by adjusting the lighting or playing some atmospheric music before starting?

Your answers will depend on a combination of circumstances, and *you* are the best person to judge.

Telling the tale

The first telling of a new story in class is probably the most exciting. There may well be some hesitation and some parts left out, but story listeners are forgiving. Your students may sense that something new is being created and they will appreciate the fact that they are receiving the story directly from you.

After all, being told a story is like being given a gift, as we said earlier.
- If you get stuck, you don't need to hide it from your students.
- Just pause, and breathe, and let the images come back to your mind.

As you tell the same story to more classes, it will become more fluent – but don't let your telling become *too* polished.
- It's worth striving to keep that freshness and spontaneity which comes with the first telling.
- It's worth adding something new each time you tell the story, whether it is prepared or spontaneous.

If you try to listen to yourself telling the story through your students' ears, the story will be created anew every time.

Telling techniques

That said, your storytelling techniques *will* develop as you tell stories in class. Making the most of your voice, body and face, as well as repetition, interaction and use of props, are among techniques outlined in the section beginning on page 25 – and then 'illustrated' in Part B in the context of the stories in this book.

In fact, the majority of the stories inevitably involve a *combination* of techniques – but you might bear in mind the following two points in *all* the stories you tell.

1 All good stories contain a grain of *truth* – to be discovered by the listener: '*When asked by young listeners if the fairy story they have just told is true, some storytellers say "It was true while I was telling it to you".*' [17]

This holds the key to the various techniques of effective storytelling – *believing* in the process, on the part of the teller and the listener too: when both are giving their full attention to the story as it unfolds.

2 Individual listeners experience stories in a rich variety of different ways. The significance of mental imagery – in other words, sensory perceptions inside listeners' minds – has been brought home to me most strikingly in workshops led by Mario Rinvolucri.
- Most listeners describe visualising mental pictures of scenes from the story, either still or moving, either in brightly-coloured or colourless tones, either in or out of focus.
- More auditory people will tune into the rhythms and sounds of the story.
- Others will feel close to the action of the story and identify themselves in a deeply kinaesthetic way with the main character.
- Many people experience *different* moments from *different* stories through *different* sensory channels.

To enhance the *experience* of a story, try referring to different senses in the words you choose – as well as providing stimuli for these senses through movement, gesture, voice modulation, percussion, music, chanting … and song.

Storytelling and the learner

'*Once upon a time, …*' immediately transports listeners to a different reality, and puts them in a relaxed, open and attentive frame of mind, primed to interpret and learn from the metaphors in the ensuing story. But how they respond to a story, and what they learn, is largely internal and therefore invisible to the storyteller.

Personal responses

Listeners' responses will be triggered by a variety of factors, such as personal experience, mood and attitude to the storyteller, as well as to other listeners and the environment.

- There may be parts of a story that a listener will miss because of internal or external distractions. The only thing you can be sure of is that no two students will experience the story identically.
- However, some clues to the listeners' personal responses to parts of a story can be noticed in sounds – such as laughter, exclamations, vocalisations – and facial expressions and body language.

As is a tale, so is life: not how long it is, but how good it is, is what matters.
Seneca

Each telling of a story can be thought of as a metaphorical 'case study' which brings the listeners' critical thinking skills into play: *'The rush of intoxication a good story triggers … makes us willing pupils, primed to absorb the myriad lessons each story imparts.'* [18]

Your listeners evaluate characters' actions, anticipate what may happen next and are constantly amending their guesses as the story develops. You can begin to get a sense of their hidden responses while you are telling the story, by inviting them to talk about their predictions or give advice to characters as the story unfolds.

Creative responses

Listeners experience stories on both a personal and emotional level, and sometimes it is enough just to leave time and space at the end of a story for them to reflect, as Barton and Booth explain: *'Letting the story settle into the landscape of individual imagination may be quite sufficient.'* [19]

How potent is the fancy!
Geoffrey Chaucer

However, what people learn from a story is not what happens in the story but in their *response* to it:

- Some students imagine richly-textured visual images while being told a story, and may even describe the experience as like watching a film in their mind's eye.
- Others may feel they are actually *in* the story and able to touch characters, objects and places. They may even, at times, *become* the protagonist.

And students are usually interested in comparing what they imagine and their own interpretations with their fellow listeners. This exchange deepens and enriches their own experience of the story.

Creative tasks

It makes sense, therefore, for students to do creative tasks after listening – and sometimes before – rather than detailed literary analysis or comprehension checking. Creative response tasks tend to focus on mental imagery, personal interpretation and the students making connections with their own experiences.

- These may involve listeners expressing what they imagine individually – by talking or writing about the story, drawing, painting or making models of characters and events, or retelling the story.
- Equally, all this can be expressed by pairs or groups of learners: *'With the teacher's careful intervention, collaborative response can grow from activities that extend the personal response and help generate a wider and more thoughtful appreciation of the story.'* [20] This involves the learners in listening attentively to each other and engaging with each other's creative ideas – for example, through comparing responses, doing roleplay and collaborative retelling.

When learning creatively and collaboratively, as Alida Gersie observes, students soon *'lose their inhibitions about trying out new ideas. They grow to enjoy themselves. Surprise and wonder at the richness of our inner worlds is often voiced. This experience is of course in itself deeply satisfying. Because so much of the work is focused around giving and receiving'.* [21]

When learners share their imaginative responses to a story they have been told together, trust is quickly built up between them – so there is a strong sense of group cohesion and confidence.

Creative collaboration

Students can, as Barton and Booth point out, make the most of *'strategies that will encourage peer talk, ... strategies that will encourage [them] to listen to each other and respond to each other's answers by building on them [and to be] concerned with the class as a group, as a community. After an experience of story, there are many learning opportunities that must not be passed up'.* [22]

When doing creative tasks before, during or after storytelling, your students can be encouraged to do the following – as suggested by Alida Gersie [23]:
- Encourage a free flow of ideas and value every contribution.
- Enjoy and recognise different ways of doing a task.
- Allow for and acknowledge different and unexpected responses.
- Show genuine interest in one another's contributions.
- Make sure all the group members have an equal share of time and attention.

Story is a medicine which strengthens and arights the individual and the community.

Clarissa Pinkola Estes

It is the most natural thing in the world for students to listen to their teacher or to each other telling a story – and then to reciprocate by telling another story they want to share. Giving them the opportunity to develop their own storytelling skills results in increased memory skills, language development, confidence in public speaking and fluency.

'[Student] storytellers ... play with the devices of the oral tradition of metre, rhythm, rhyme and repetition, and experiment with tones of voice and the rhythms of words as well as the ideas, issues and meanings in the tale. This opportunity to explore the latent possibilities of the human voice, its inflection, emphasis, cadence and the use of pause, is a useful one ... Speaking and listening [are] enhanced ... [Students learn] to hear the colour, the drama and the emotive engagement in the sounds that words and language offer.' [24]

There is an example from my own experience, relating to the traditional Welsh folk tale *The Shepherd of the Myddvai.* (There is a video of me telling it on YouTube.)
- This story has a universal theme, recognisable to any culture: the human falling in love with a being from another world.
- When I told the tale to a group of Korean business students along with their wives and children at a social event, they were reminded of a Korean tale in which a woodcutter saves the life of a hunted deer which then shows him the mountain lake where the fairy maidens from the skies go to bathe.

Both tales involve marriage, broken promises and eventual separation and heartbreak. Without any preparation, Young Eun Kim, who teaches English to young learners in Korea, stood up and told the tale – in English – while the rest of the group supported her and added in the details she missed or was unsure of. In essence, it was a collaborative telling.

Which brings us on to the subject of storytelling in the language classroom.

Storytelling and language learning

'Story telling is a uniquely powerful linguistic and psychological technique in the hands of a language teacher which s/he can use with people of any culture ... and with people of virtually any age.' [25]

Benefits

If you are teaching a foreign language to your whole class, or if some of the students in your class are non-native speakers, storytelling is ideal for building language learners' self-confidence and developing their language skills. Language teachers are generally capable of becoming good storytellers and your students will benefit enormously from being told stories in the target language.

Your tale, sir, would cure deafness.

William Shakespeare

I realised for the first time how effective storytelling in language teaching could be in the early 1990s, when storyteller Mike Dunstan visited the young learners programme I was teaching on at the Isca School of English in Exeter, UK. I was astounded that, for a whole hour of storytelling in English, he could hold the attention of thirty young learners who spoke a variety of different first languages. The students sat entranced and followed the stories as he told them.

Mike didn't seem to modify the language he used, because simple folk tales are told most effectively using uncomplicated structures and vocabulary. *'Fairy stories … are often familiar in outline'* as John Morgan and Mario Rinvolucri tell us: *'the language is simple yet the meanings are evocative and many-layered.'* [26]

- There are universal features in the structure of traditional tales and, given that the students were familiar with the underlying structure, this clearly supported their understanding.
- It is likely that the students were in the same relaxed and attentive story-listening frame of mind as when listening to and enjoying stories in their mother tongue at home or at school in their own country.

And non-native language teachers are just as capable as mother-tongue teachers of telling stories to their students – as those students are of listening to them. As Morgan and Rinvolucri put it in their resource book for teachers of English *Once Upon a Time*, *'the communicative gain will at least outweigh the un-Englishness you may hear in your telling'.* [27]

- If you have the same mother tongue as your students and are teaching what, for you as well, is a second language, then you are a perfect language learning model for your students.
- Your students can aspire to be, one day, as good a user of the target language as you.

Beliefs

After a few years' experience of storytelling in language teaching, I was fortunate to be invited to spend a week in the south of Italy, doing a project with elementary learners of English in technical and professional schools in rural Basilicata.

- For many of the students, this was their first experience of meeting a native English speaker, and it was clear in each of the one- and two-hour storytelling sessions I did that, at the outset, most of them didn't expect to understand much at all.
- Some of the teachers also doubted that their students would be able to follow the stories without simultaneous translation from them.

In fact, the quality of attention the students paid to the storytelling was remarkable. They instantly followed the first and simplest story and, by the end of the session, they were able to demonstrate that they had at least got the gist of each of the subsequent stories.

Evidence of this was that they were able to retell one story in pairs in Italian, and pairs of students successfully re-enacted scenes from another story. This storytelling experience challenged the students' and the teachers' beliefs that the students would not be able to deal with an extended piece of foreign language spoken by a native speaker.

Interaction

Perhaps you too have had the experience of being told a story in a language you are learning, and felt that you understood more than you expected. If the story is told from the heart, it seems as if there's some magic going on. As we said, this can partly be explained by the familiar structures and simple language used in folk tales, and the relaxed and attentive learning mode the listeners are in. However, there are more factors involved:

- When students are in a language learning classroom, they are used to being set written tasks to complete while doing listening activities, which means that they break eye contact with the teacher who is speaking to them.
- When students are required to listen to audio recordings, there is an even greater distancing, because there is no opportunity to interact with the speaker.

A major advantage of storytelling with students you teach regularly is that your knowledge of them helps you to modify the way you tell a story and pitch it 'just right'. You can engage

If you don't know the trees you may be lost in the forest, but if you don't know the stories you may be lost in life.

Siberian Elder

Always tell what you feel.

Gabriel García Márquez

directly with them and modify how you tell the story, in response to the behaviour of the learners in front of you. Morgan and Rinvolucri write: '*To be told a story by a live storyteller involves one in 'I–thou' listening, where the listeners can directly influence the telling.*' [28]

Communication

Students are listening, then, to a real and present person. The 'live story' experience involves picking up on non-verbal language, both for teller and listener. It influences, and is influenced by, the relationship between the students and their teacher.

The storytelling language teacher who makes the most of using body language, facial expression, mime, gesture, props – and all the other subtleties of interpersonal communication – can make comprehension easier for their learners, while making the story more engaging for everyone.

- The way you modulate your voice is different when you are face-to-face with your listeners and responding to their responses.
- The cadences, rhythms and emotions expressed in the voice of the interacting storytelling teacher are altered when students are looking at you and responding directly to you.

Your willingness to reveal your 'storyteller self' to your students will deepen interpersonal trust and sharing in the classroom, and is likely to lead to increased risk-taking by your students in the target language.

Imagination

Mental imagery is given free rein when we create a safe and comfortable atmosphere in which students can listen openly. To quote Jane Arnold, Herbert Puchta and Mario Rinvolucri: '*They will be able to comprehend the gist of the story better if during the listening process they are able to build a full representation of the story in their mind … with visual images of the people and objects in the story, with auditory representations of people's voices, environmental sounds and so forth.*' [29]

This happens more naturally as storytelling becomes integral to classroom language learning:

- Each story will have its own vividly imagined story space for each student
- Each student will '*move around in that space, feel imagined body sensations … or even imagine the smell or taste of things suggested by the mental representations*'. [30]

Storytelling and the language learner

The co-creative nature of storytelling has a positive impact on students' language learning. The main challenge to language learners understanding a story you tell is likely to be the vocabulary you use. Storytelling is ideal for introducing and revising language items, because folk tales are rich in content and therefore the words are contextualised.

Vocabulary

Too much unfamiliar vocabulary can be a barrier to students following the story. Generally, it is easy to limit the amount of *new* vocabulary you use in a story – by sticking to simpler high-frequency items.

- If you do need to use unfamiliar vocabulary, it may be because it is essential to the story and the students do need to understand it.
- Alternatively, you might consciously include unknown vocabulary because of the poetry of the sound and/or the meaning of the word. You'd like your students to be able to hear some expressive words and be comfortable with the idea that they will not understand them all and that it is beneficial for them to listen without catching one hundred percent of the meaning. After all, this is normal in language learning.

If new vocabulary is essential to the meaning of the story, you need to choose whether you are going to familiarise the students with it *before* you tell the story, or whether you can make it clear to them in context *while* telling the story.

- A short task in which key vocabulary is introduced prior to telling the story can be useful (see *Cloud Eating* on page 63).
- Using mime during the telling can help to make vocabulary clear (see *Manju* on page 47).

You could also use sounds or simple props – but avoid relying on pictures, as they are likely to have too much influence on the students' own mental images. If you do need to use a picture, consider doing a very simple line drawing which leaves a lot of space for the imagination. There is a strong link between language, emotion and mental imagery.

'*Mental imagery can improve comprehension and recall,*' as Arnold, Puchta and Rinvolucri say, '*language material is processed more deeply through the use of imagery and is stored in a more permanent manner. In fact we could say that images are essential for us to get meaning out of language.*' [31]

- Students are likely to want to use the same key vocabulary themselves in creative activities *after* listening to the story.
- This would be a good time to support them – by inviting them to say the new vocabulary in the context of a phrase from the story, so that they are aware of common collocations and are confident about the pronunciation.

One final thought, here – if *you* were lucky enough to be told stories as a child, think how much of *your* mother tongue vocabulary *you* learnt in this way.

Extended listening

Language learners are highly engaged when being told a story, and this leads to raised levels of confidence in their listening skills. The fact that people are hardwired for stories, and that storytelling is live and interactive, means that students understand far more, and are able to concentrate for longer, in comparison with any other kinds of listening they do.

Creative listening

Pronunciation in a second language is learnt primarily through listening and noticing how the sounds of the target language are produced. The extended listening that storytelling offers is ideal. Students are listening creatively as they tune into rhythm, intonation, tempo, connected speech and pausing.

- The fact that they are looking at their teacher means that they are also picking up visual information about the mechanics of the way sounds are made in the target language, and not just from the movement of the lips.
- Even though the tongue, the inside of the mouth and the vocal folds are hidden, human beings are rarely conscious of the extent to which we notice the most subtle movements.

Consider how hearing-impaired people can learn to lip-read, and how babies gaze at and imitate their parents when learning speech.

There are also abundant opportunities to involve students in participating verbally in listening to stories, particularly when you introduce repeated phrases which might be chanted or sung together.

- Students can be invited to repeat a phrase and, as the story progresses, join in together with the teacher.
- The teacher might choose to adapt the repeated phrase in order to give the students practice of a particular pronunciation feature, as well as to consolidate new vocabulary.

This kind of repetition is a key feature of language acquisition, providing scaffolding which enables listeners to internalise new language. Barton and Booth point out that when students join in, '*the story, borne on the playful and imaginative interchange between teller and audience, comes to life magnificently*'. [32]

Finally, retelling parts of the story afterwards gives the students the chance to activate the language features they have noticed. One of the most effective ways of learning to *tell* a story is to *listen* to it being told over and again, just as a child does.

It is not the voice that commands the story: it is the ear.

Italo Calvino

All the better to hear you with!

Jakob and Wilhelm Grimm

Extended speaking

Retelling a story builds language learners' spoken fluency and confidence.

- Initially, students tend to imitate the story you tell them, striving to use largely the same structures and vocabulary as you. This is a natural and useful stage, and promotes accurate language production.
- However, it can be restricting and unnatural to retell a story in another person's words. After all, we tell stories in our own unique way, just as we all speak differently.

When they listen to you telling a story, students will be very aware that you are not reciting from a memorised script.

- This gives you a chance to discuss the extent to which clarity in communication is more important than grammatical accuracy in oral storytelling.
- It gives you the chance to make it clear that each time a student retells a story, the story will become more and more their own version and it will vary according to the context.

Nearly all the storytelling language learners I work with comment that, when they retell a story in or outside class, it is by far the most extended piece of uninterrupted speaking they ever do in the target language. Their self-esteem flourishes when they acknowledge that they are able to tell a whole story in that language.

Creative speaking

But retelling a story is only one way in which language learners can develop their speaking skills. Storytelling offers a wide range of possibilities for creative speaking, as demonstrated by the activities in this book. Whether discussing meaning, comparing mental imagery, doing improvised drama, making predictions or sharing personal experiences, storytelling generates both extended *and* creative speaking.

- The language teacher's role becomes one of supporting and monitoring, and choosing whether to intervene and to what extent.
- When you are promoting creative expression, the only interventions needed are those which support learners in their endeavour to express themselves more effectively – for example, by helping them to reformulate or pronounce a phrase so that it is intelligible.

As Morgan and Rinvolucri say: '*For all, adequate communication is an attainable miracle, if the teacher is prepared to allow it.*' [33] And this applies to language learners at all levels.

Elementary speaking

Four months before writing this, I spent a memorable two hours with a group of twelve adult elementary learners of English from Saudi Arabia.

- I told them that they would be able to tell a five-minute story in English by the end of the class, but they were reluctant to believe me.
- I then told them a simplified version of the folk tale Arabic speakers most often tell me: *Joha and his Donkey*, featuring the same wise fool as mentioned on page 9, a story they all knew well in Arabic.

A few months earlier, I had been teaching Jawaher Mutlaq Alotaibi, an advanced learner of English from Saudi Arabia. She had contributed the story in English and Arabic to *World Stories*, a wonderful online resource I work with, so I based my storytelling on her version (*www.worldstories.org.uk/stories/story/9-joha-and-his-donkey/english*) – see page 22.

As I told *Joha and his Donkey*, I audio-recorded myself telling it on my mp3 player. It is a short wisdom tale with plenty of repetition and humour, and I used a lot of mime to support the students' comprehension.

- The students showed that they were able to understand well.
- Next, I gave these elementary learners the chance to read and listen to the same story in their mother tongue (Arabic) in order to refresh their memories of the story they knew from before – at *www.worldstories.org.uk/stories/story/9-joha-and-his-donkey/arabic*.
- After that, they worked on the recording of me telling the story, breaking it down into chunks and focusing on pronunciation.

- Then they 'stepped through the story' in pairs (see page 33).

At the end of the two-hour session, every student had told the story to a partner in English, and was able to go and tell the story to someone outside the class who had never heard it before. These students' level of self-belief in their ability to learn English was raised.

The day before writing this – in other words, four months later – one of those students, Saleh, wanted to tell the story to new Chinese, Iraqi and Kazak students in our class. He retold *Joha and his Donkey* fluently and with great enthusiasm, a sign of how engaging and memorable classroom storytelling is.

Joha and his Donkey

One day, Joha was riding upon his donkey on the way to market. Joha's son walked beside the donkey, holding the reins and talking with his father. When the father and son passed a small group of people gathered by the side of the track, the people criticised Joha. They said to the old man, 'How can you be so heartless, Joha? How can you ride upon the donkey while your son is forced to walk beside you?'

When Joha heard these words, he climbed down and lifted his son up onto the donkey's back in his place. Joha and his son continued on their journey, Joha walking beside the donkey, holding the reins as they made their way towards the market.

A mile down the road, Joha passed a small group of women gathered around a well. When the women saw Joha, they were very shocked. They asked of him, 'How is it that an old man walks while his young son rides upon the donkey? Surely this is not right!' So Joha climbed upon the donkey's back with his son, and they continued on their journey.

It was getting into the late afternoon, the sun was shining high up in the sky and it was very hot, but still Joha and his son continued on their journey towards the market. The donkey was moving very slowly because of the weight of the father and the son upon its back, but nobody criticised – until they came across a group of people gathered on the edge of the town where the market was held.

The people pointed with disapproval when they saw Joha and his son both sitting on the back of the little donkey, which was moving so slowly under the weight of the father and the son. 'Why do you both ride upon such a small donkey?' they cried out to Joha. 'Can you not see that you are too heavy and your donkey cannot support your weight?'

'I think it is best if we both get off of the donkey and walk,' Joha said to his son. 'That way, nobody can say anything to us anymore.' So Joha and his son climbed down from the donkey, Joha took the reins in order to lead the donkey and walked with his son towards the marketplace in the centre of the village.

But when Joha arrived at the marketplace, many people laughed and criticised and made fun of the old man. 'What a fool!' they declared. 'What kind of a man owns a donkey and yet walks with his son when he should be riding?'

Even if a lot of gestures and guesswork are involved when language learners tell stories, the communication is genuine and, while students are attempting to get the message across, they are often able to overcome inhibiting factors such as lack of confidence and the belief that their limited vocabulary prevents them from succeeding in extended speaking tasks.

- They already know the content of the story they are telling, so their focus is not on what to *say*, but on how best to enable the listeners to *understand* and *enjoy* it.
- Even elementary students are able to tell a story without written prompts, as long as the teacher manages to establish a safe environment and a supportive atmosphere.

Storytelling and learner development

I often teach classes of mixed-nationality young adult students part-time over two months. They are preparing for academic study at university level in the UK.

- Within the first two weeks, they all learn basic storytelling techniques and are able to tell a short tale they have learnt from me. For most of them, it is their first time telling a folk tale in English.
- By the end of two months, each student has confidently told a short folk tale to the whole class. I have learnt several of the stories in this book from students in this way!

In their end-of-course evaluation, they generally comment as follows:

- They feel that they have developed in confidence, fluency, pronunciation and using vocabulary in English through storytelling.
- They feel they are more able to give a successful *academic* presentation, using many of their storytelling skills – such as using body language and eye contact, speaking without referring to notes and organising ideas.

The students are mostly from across Asia and already know how to tell a large number of folk tales in their mother tongue, because such tales feature centrally in their education and upbringing. Doing storytelling in this way – as part of their formal academic studies – means that they are playing to their strengths.

Let me conclude with a final 'story':

I was teaching Deok, a young Korean man, one-to-one. After telling him *The Tale of Ivan*, a traditional story from Cornwall of a young man who travels abroad to seek his fortune and then faces a series of dilemmas, he reciprocated by telling a traditional Korean tale about how, long ago, families were forced to face a far greater dilemma: whether to abandon their elderly relatives in the mountains to die, as demanded by law, or to face the penalty of the entire family being executed.

In the tale, an old man is saved from this terrible fate and hidden away by his son. The old man's wisdom saves the Korean nation, and finally the cruel law is repealed.

- It was a struggle for Deok to recall the finer details of a story he had heard many years before, but he succeeded in telling the whole tale.
- His ten-minute telling was the most extended piece of uninterrupted speech he achieved during the course.
- Just afterwards, he remarked on the boost to his self-esteem as an English speaker.

His story made a powerful impact on me – the seriousness of his telling and the evident pride in his native culture transcended any linguistic barriers.

- I retold the story I had learnt from Deok a week later – to a large audience of teachers from all over the world at the IATEFL Conference in Harrogate.
- During my telling, one of the Korean teachers present was able to supply some of the details Deok had forgotten.

The fact was: I was retelling a story I had recently heard, and I was telling it in the true oral storytelling tradition, and this was possibly the main reason why the audience responded so warmly to it.

Bibliography

1 Gersie, A *Earthtales* Green Print 1992 (no longer in print)

2 Damasio, A *Self Comes to Mind: Constructing the Conscious Brain* Pantheon 2011

3 Cron, L *Wired for Story* Ten Speed Press (Random House) 2012

4 Pinker, S *How the Mind Works* Penguin 1999

5 Propp, V 'The Morphology of the Folktale' *http://citeseerx.ist.psu.edu/viewdoc/download?doi =10.1.1.133.1322&rep=rep1&type=pdf*

6 Wright, A 'The Place of Stories in ELT' In Paran, A and Watts, E (Eds) *Storytelling in ELT* IATEFL 2003

7 Barton, B and Booth, D *Stories in the Classroom* Pembroke Publishers 1990

8 Wajnryb, R *Stories* Cambridge University Press 2003

9 Barton, B and Booth, D op. cit.

10 Stephens, G J, Silbert, L J and Hasson, U 'Speaker–listener neural coupling underlies successful communication' *Proceedings of the National Academy of Sciences of the United States of America* 107 (32) Retrieved 12 May 2013 from *www.pnas.org/content/107/32/14425.full?sid= c8205d6a-08c1-463f-9e38-b496c4da*

11 Wajnryb, R op. cit.

12 Heathfield, D 'Storytelling for Bridging Cultures' *Modern English Teacher* 16 (1)

13 Rinvolucri, M 'Story telling: the language teacher's oldest technique' *http://www.teachingenglish.org.uk/articles* 19 November 2008

14 Davies, A *Storytelling in the Classroom* Paul Chapman Pubishing 2007

15 From an online lecture by Prof. Eric Rabkin of the University of Michigan – in the Coursera course 'Fantasy and Science Fiction in the Modern World'

16 Bilbrough, N 'De-humanising Language Teaching? Painting by Numbers' *www.hltmag.co.uk*

17 Heathfield, D 'A Storytelling Experience' *English Teaching Professional* 63

18 Cron, L op. cit.

19 Barton, B and Booth, D op. cit.

20 Barton, B and Booth, D ibid.

21 Gersie, A op. cit.

22 Barton, B and Booth, D op. cit.

23 Gersie, A op. cit.

24 Grainger, T *Traditional Storytelling in the Primary Classroom* Scholastic 1997

25 Rinvolucri, M op. sit

26 Morgan, J and Rinvolucri, M *Once Upon a Time* Cambridge University Press 1983

27 Morgan, J and Rinvolucri, M ibid.

28 Morgan, J and Rinvolucri, M ibid.

29 Arnold, J, Puchta, H and Rinvolucri, M *Imagine That!* Helbling Languages 2007

30 Arnold, J, Puchta, H and Rinvolucri, M ibid.

31 Arnold, J, Puchta, H and Rinvolucri, M ibid.

32 Barton, B and Booth, D op. cit.

33 Morgan, J and Rinvolucri, M op. cit.

Telling techniques for telling tales

Chapter One

The teacher as storyteller

Voice ...

This reference section is divided into three parts, following the three chapters in Part B of this book – although it is obvious that there are no watertight 'divisions' possible. For example:

- There are suggestions for you, the *teacher*, to use your voice to maximum effect, which in turn will influence your facial expressions as well as your body language.
- And you will be amazed how your *students*, as storytellers themselves, will – with your support and example – develop their very own skills across a wide range of these 'telling' techniques.

What follows are details of various techniques to guide both you and your students towards successful storytelling. These techniques will be reprised very briefly – as a reminder, and to focus your attention – in the context of all of the stories and their accompanying procedures throughout Part B of *Storytelling With Our Students*.

Make the most of your voice in your storytelling – it is your main tool!

The narrator's voice

The key to modulating your voice pitch and volume is to breathe comfortably through your chest.

Breathing

Before telling a story, it's a good idea to do breathing and voice warm-up exercises. For example:

- Make a different extended vowel sound as you breathe out, each time making the sound last longer than the previous time.
- Let your voice vibrate in your chest as you hum a tune at the lower pitch of your speaking voice.
- Choose a phrase from the story you are going to tell, and say it in as many different ways as possible: whispering across a crowded room, singing opera, making a public announcement, saying it while laughing, in a mouse's squeal, in a lion's growl …

Modulating

Playfully modulate the pitch, tempo and volume of your voice as you rehearse a story. For example:

- A higher-pitched voice, an increased tempo and a higher volume can be used separately or in combination to communicate a rapid sequence of actions, and to convey urgency or excitement.
- A lower-pitched voice, a slower tempo and a lower volume can convey a sense of mystery or deeply-felt emotion, such as love or sorrow.

Avoid modulating your voice too much in class, or your subtle storytelling will turn into melodrama.

Of course, voice and body language (see below on page 26) *in combination* express emotion and attitude, so they need to be rehearsed together.

See page 40:
The Story of Sidwell

The characters' voices

It works well to use direct speech when you tell a folk tale.

Hearing the characters' own words has an impact on the listener and adds more variety to the storytelling.

Your characters' voices can be similar to, or quite different from, your own normal speaking voice. The more 'extreme' the character, the more the voice is likely to differ from your own – in terms of features such as the following:
- Speech pattern
- Pitch
- Tempo
- Accent
- Volume

As you rehearse telling a story, experiment freely with different voices.
- You will soon settle on one that feels right for a character.
- It is almost inevitable that your *posture* and *facial expressions* will also change – along with your voice.

See page 42:
The Dog and the Wolf

Face and body ...

Always be aware of how *you* are communicating physically in your storytelling – your *listeners* will certainly notice.

Facial expression
Your facial expression and your voice are completely interlinked.

Your face becomes more animated than usual whenever you are telling a story. The slightest raising of an eyebrow or pout of the lips can completely transform the meaning of your words, whether you are speaking as the narrator or as a character – such is the power of facial expression in storytelling.

The story will come across in a very different way:
- If you tell a story with a neutral, impassive face.
- If you tell the *same* story with an animated face, showing strong emotions.

Even if the listeners have their eyes closed!

The way you express yourself with eyes, mouth and angle of the head will depend on the nature of the story:
- A humorous action-packed story may demand more exaggerated facial expressions.
- A simple short wisdom tale is more suited to more moderate, but still animated, facial expressions.

Often, within the telling of a single tale, it is a good idea to move between the two. And, naturally, when speaking the words of a *character*, your facial expressions are likely to be more distinctive.

See page 44:
The Village of Fools

Body language
When you tell a story, you say as much with your body as you do with your face, your voice and your choice of words.

Remaining very still can draw your listeners in – just as much as moving expressively.

Each person has their own physical storytelling presence. However, you can make your body language vary from story to story, and this depends largely on how you want the story to come across:
- You might stand and move around, when telling stories with a lot of physical action.
- You might sit motionless, when telling more reflective wisdom tales and parables.

And within the same story, you can have moments of stillness and moments of lively movement.

Make any movements and gestures definite and purposeful:
- They may be as subtle as a shrug of the shoulders.
- They may be as big as running fast on the spot.

Try watching me tell the Australian creation myth *Ngaardi and Toonkoo* on YouTube – with the sound turned off.

See page 45:
Ngaardi and Toonkoo

Mime
Many of us use mime unconsciously to hold the attention of friends and colleagues – and to add emphasis to what we say in everyday conversation – so it comes naturally to use mime *even more* to help our students understand us in class.
- Mimed actions make storytelling more entertaining – as well as easier for the students to follow.
- They also make things easier to join in with – both physically and verbally.

It would be excessive to mime every single object and event in a story – this would almost certainly distract your listeners:
- Decide in advance *what* you are going to mime – for emphasis, and to support comprehension.
- Rehearse these mimed actions very carefully.

Generally, a brief, simple, easily recognisable mime using your hands is sufficient, but occasionally exaggerating a mime can add to a comic story – for example, using both hands to pull on an imaginary rope could be exaggerated by leaning back and grimacing.
- You can invite the students to join in with a repeated *phrase*, but you can also get them to do repeated *actions* with you.
- You can also encourage them to do both together – an excellent way of reinforcing language kinaesthetically.

See page 46:
Manju

Accompaniment ...

Sound deeply affects story listeners – often unconsciously – and has done so since before we were even born.

The sound of music

Live music, song, percussion and sound effects can add hugely to live storytelling. There is a blurred line between sounds, percussion, music and song in the way I and many others do storytelling.

- Personally, I don't advocate pre-recorded background music except in story *making* or creative storytelling.
- See the YouTube videos referenced in the 'Sources' section on page 122 – sounds are used very differently in each.

You can also sing a repeated rhyme or phrase, and invite your students to sing with you.

Musical accompaniment can be incorporated on any number of storytelling occasions, but it is also the subject of one of the stories in Chapter One of *Storytelling With Our Students*.

See page 48:
Filling the House

Sound effects

Bells, shakers and drums from around the world fill shelves in my home:

- Different ones are used with different stories I tell.
- I accompany myself during *certain parts* of a story, rather than *throughout* the narrative.

You might think about using sound effects yourself – or consider getting your students involved:

- Invite one or more students to accompany you – either with or without rehearsal beforehand.
- Invite the students to tap on their knees and softly howl – to create 'storm' sound effects, for example.
- Invite all the students to clap their hands or shake shakers in rhythm together – to emphasise a chorally repeated rhyme.

See page 84:
Mbongoro

Repetition ...

Our brains tune in naturally to the rhythmic speech patterns which are often repeated in oral storytelling.

Words

At the simplest level, a key word – mostly an action verb –

can be repeated three times to add emphasis and get the students joining in, particularly when the same word appears over and over in the course of a story.

- The students are likely to recall this rhythmically repeated word and say it together with you.
- You can encourage them to do so with a simple signal – slow down and then pause for a moment and smile at the students, opening your hands out towards them as an invitation to join in.

See page 50:
Maui and the Big Fish

Phrases

In the same way as words, whole phrases are often repeated chorally during storytelling, and students are generally eager to join in – as long as you invite them with confidence.

Frequent and playful repetition of chunks of language in the meaningful context of a story is one of the most effective ways of learning language.

In traditional stories around the world, things tend to happen in threes. For example: *Goldilocks and the Three Bears*, *The Three Little Pigs* and *The Three Billy Goats Gruff*.

- The first time you say the repeated phrase, pause for a moment beforehand, lean towards the students and say it with slightly increased volume. You might or might not invite the students – with a gesture – to repeat the phrase *after you*.
- The second time you come to the repeated phrase, pause again and, with open hands, invite the students to say it *together with you*.
- The third time, pause, make the same gesture of invitation and, if your students are ready, let them say the phrase *while you remain silent*.

You can use the same repeated phrase as the one you learnt when you first came across the story.

- Alternatively, you can change it for a particular phrase that you'd like your students to practise saying.
- Another option is simply to create your own phrase for a story – where events are repeated three or more times.

Nearly all the repeated phrases in the stories I tell are ones I have adapted or made up myself.

Repeating in this way not only helps the students remember the *meaning* of the phrase but also, by saying it with you, they internalise the *speech pattern* and the *pronunciation*.

See page 52:
Anansi and Tiger

Phrases with different words

It is both challenging and fun for students to remember and repeat phrases which change each time they are repeated.

A good example is the well-known story of Goldilocks, which includes large amounts of repetition:
Who's been eating my porridge?
Who's been sitting on my chair?
Who's been sleeping in my bed?

The repeated phrase provides a framework for the students, and this allows for experimenting with variations within the framework.

See page 54:
Lazy Jack

Rhymes

Another way of repeating a phrase is in the form of a rhyme – where the speech pattern is heightened and rhythmic.
There is usually a repetition, as follows:
- In the pattern of stressed syllables.
- Of the final sounds in each rhyming line.

For example, in 'Snow White':
Mirror Mirror on the wall,
Who is the fairest of us all?

Rhymes are an enjoyable way for students to play with and remember language sounds and rhythms, and are common in folk tales.

But why not make up your own repeated rhymes for your students to join in with?

See page 56:
Juan and the Magic Tree

Episodes

Where whole episodes are repeated three times almost word for word, such as in *The Three Little Pigs*, you can encourage your students to tell the story along with you – even if it's the first time they are hearing it.
- Tell the first episode clearly and rhythmically.
- Signal to the students when the repetition of the episode starts.
- Encourage them to say what they can, along with you.

Avoid slowing the tempo down – rather, let the students try to keep up with you.

When the episode begins a third time, the students may be able to tell the story chorally in time with you.
- This builds their confidence in their story *learning* and story *telling* skills.
- It also supports their learning of larger chunks of language and the features of extended speech, such as sentence stress, intonation and word boundaries.

See page 58:
The Witch of Tavistock

Interacting ...

Storytelling has always been a communal experience – it is therefore natural for listeners to interact with a story as it is being told.

With the characters

A simple and effective technique is to step into the role of a main character while you tell a story – and interact with the students from within that role. This gives them an opportunity to engage imaginatively with the story as it is being told to them.

The students can be asked to step into role along with you. For example:
- As villagers, giving a character advice.
- As members of a jury, arguing over a character's guilt.
- As voices inside a character's head, evaluating the relative merits of different courses of action.

See page 60:
Bedd Gelert

With the students

While telling a story, it's a good idea to be flexible and be prepared to respond to your students. You can interact directly with them:
- Ask them to advise what a character should do.
- Ask them for a solution to a problem in the story.
- Ask them to make predictions about events in the story or how the story will end.

Try to ensure that the interaction is *integral* to the storytelling and does not *interrupt* the story (but see below for an interesting exception):
- Make sure you keep this interaction brief.
- Make sure that all the students in the class listen closely to each other's contributions.

There may even be opportunities for carefully managed discussion between the students themselves.

See page 62:
How to Weigh an Elephant

Through interruptions

This is a quite different way of telling a story, which involves being continuously quizzed about the story – as you tell it. The quizzing can actually make the storytelling more spontaneous, energetic and entertaining.
- You set a short time limit.
- You challenge the students to stop you from finishing the tale by constantly asking you questions.
- You answer any questions that are relevant to the story.

- You ignore any questions that try to catch you out.

In other words, the questions should enhance the storytelling rather than spoil it.

Generally, the students enjoy the opportunity to 'outdo' their teacher, and they will manage to prevent you from finishing the tale.

Finally, you tell the tale a second time from start to finish – without being interrupted.

- You incorporate some of the details that emerged from answering the students' questions.
- This gives them a real sense of contributing and participating in the storytelling process.

See page 63:
Cloud Eating

Through riddles

Riddles are a feature of folk tales in many different cultures, and they are popular with logical and lateral thinkers – who enjoy trying to work out the solution.

- Often there will be one student who calls out the solution to the riddle before the others have even had a chance to think about it.
- Often you can avoid this problem by asking the students to whisper the solution to a partner, or to write it down.

If the riddle in the story does not need to be solved immediately, you can let the students work it out while you go on telling the story – and then let them voice their guesses, just before the solution is actually given.

See page 64:
A Question of Brains

Through different cultures

When students hear traditional stories from different cultures:

- They notice that people from other cultures have values, experiences and concerns which are similar to their own.
- They realise that all cultures have their own unique characteristics, which give a strong sense of identity.

Noticing similarities between tales which come from two different cultures – but have similar features – heightens the students' intercultural awareness.

See page 66:
The Three Golden Hairs and **Jackal and the Shining Child**

Through personalisation

Some of the simplest traditional tales hold up a mirror to us, so that our own weaknesses (and occasionally our strengths) are revealed. It is often possible for the students to find personal stories from their own experiences which are reflected in these tales.

To introduce this notion, you can adapt and personalise a traditional tale:

- You tell it so that your students believe that it actually happened to *you*.
- Alternatively, you can actually tell a *true* story about yourself, based on the tale.

See page 68:
The Lost Axe

Chapter Two

Creative ways into and out of a story

Leading in and out ...

A story is told most effectively when it is integral to – and adds to – a wider creative learning experience.

For almost every topic that the students are likely to study in class, there is a suitable short folk tale which can be an effective lead-in or summing-up.

The subject matter of folk tales is so wide-ranging, lending itself to intercurricular teaching (see page 112 in Part C) or to more general discussion.

Here are just four examples from Chapter Three in Part B:

- *The Bridge* (see page 97) can introduce topics related to relationships, faith, peace and war.
- *How Spider Got a Narrow Waist* (page 101) fits in with the theme of food.
- *Sand and Stone* (page 103) links well to topics related to friendship and forgiveness.
- *After the Fire* (page 91) can be told as a lead-in to studying topics related to the environment.

Folk tales tend to be simple in *form* but many-layered in *meaning* – and the students tend to be very focused and use their imaginations while listening.

- A lead-in story stimulates student creativity and responsiveness to a new topic.
- A summing-up story can put the students in a reflective frame of mind, and help them digest what they have been learning about the topic.

See page 70:
The Teacher

Leading in ...

Before your students even listen to a story, you can encourage them to anticipate, imagine and be creative.

Predicting

Giving the students the opportunity to predict what might happen in a story develops creative thinking and focuses their attention when you tell the story. They will base their predictions on the information you choose to give them.

This information could be any of the following:
- Just the title.
- An overview of the plot.
- The opening of the story.
- A couple of clues.

Alternatively, you could invite them to base their prediction on sensory clues:
- Showing them pictures.
- Passing them objects to handle.
- Getting them to listen to sounds or music.
- Giving them things to smell or taste.

See page 71:
Little Dog, Panther and Monkey

Imagining

A more in-depth way of getting students to make predictions about a story is to let them quiz you about it, and then use their imaginations to tell their own versions – before they listen.
- The fact that they have already made up their own story will affect the way they listen.
- They will be comparing the version you tell with their own imagined version.

See page 72:
The Small Bird's Wisdom

Improvising

You can give the students advance information about the main characters and key events in a short and simple story, or in a key episode within a story.
- You can ask them to do an improvised drama roleplay, based on that information.
- They then listen to you telling the story.
- This will focus them on comparing the story with the one they have created beforehand.

See page 74:
Aldar Kose Tricks the Bai

Leading out ...

Once they have listened to the story, your students are ready to respond creatively.

A tableau

One of the simplest and most powerful drama techniques involves the students making still and silent images with their bodies which represent a moment frozen in time.
- These are called 'tableaux'.
- Tableaux are, typically, exaggerated – to accentuate the action and emotion, and to explore a dramatic moment.

A simple tableau can be made by an individual student, but when two or more students make a tableau together, the relationship between them can provide a more complex and interesting image to explore.
- *One* character might be represented by *one* student.
- *One* dragon-character, for example, could be composed of *two or more* bodies.
- Large *inanimate* objects – tables, bridges, even forests – can be represented by at least two students working together.

After listening to a story, the students can be invited to look at each other's tableaux:
- Which moment is being depicted?
- What might happen next?

A tableau can also be a starting point for a piece of drama improvisation.

See page 76:
Dongguo and the Wolf

A roleplay

Acting out a story is the essence of all drama, and it comes naturally to most students. It develops a greater understanding of characters' viewpoints, as well as developing language and movement skills. In a roleplay, the students explore the story by experiencing it 'from the inside'.
- It can be done with or without dialogue.
- It can be done in pairs or in groups.
- It can be scripted or improvised.
- It can be very brief, or extended over a longer period.

See page 78:
The Coat

An interview

The students can explore the inner world of a character, by being interviewed in role at a given moment in the story.
- Initially, it is a good idea for the *teacher* to interview one student. You first ask them to imagine and describe the character from the outside in a sensory way.

- You then carefully guide them to talk – in role as the character – about their behaviour and motivation.
- Then another student can be interviewed in role by the *other students* – with the teacher facilitating, in order to guide the interview in a constructive way.

After that, the students might be ready to do further interviews on their own in small groups.

See page 80:
Garuda and Turtle

A task

The students can be offered the choice of writing or drawing what they have imagined while being told a story – particularly if they prefer not to talk about it straight away.
- Teachers are frequently accustomed to setting *all* the students the *same* writing task or the same drawing task.
- When given an *option*, the students are freer to express themselves as they wish, and this is likely to result in a higher degree of creativity.

Once the tasks are complete, exploring each other's creative responses through the different media offers deeper insight into the story and into each other's perspectives.
- Written responses might include messages, prose, songs, poetry or letters.
- Drawing responses could be cartoons, portraits, details, landscapes or abstract images.
- Other creative responses could be other forms of artwork, music, dance or drama.

See page 82:
The Snowgirl

A gift

The simple act of choosing a gift for a character gives the students a chance to interact with a story in different ways.
- Some may choose a *practical object* as a gift.
- Others may explore more deeply, and select *symbolic* gifts, personal *qualities* or life *skills*.

Acting out the ritual of presenting and receiving gifts, and finding out about other students' ideas, can illuminate unnoticed aspects of the story, its characters and its meanings. The gift can be chosen at the end of the story. However:
- The students might want the character to receive the gift at the point in the story where it would have been of greatest benefit.
- Alternatively, you can pause in a story and invite the students to say what gift they would give the character at that point – before you continue.

See page 84:
Mbongoro

A personal response

Questions can give students a framework to express their personal responses to a story. However:
- Different students will want to express different things.
- A wide *range* of questions to choose from and respond to will make this easier for them.
- Questions which lead to a multitude of different personal responses are more interesting than 'right or wrong' questions which simply test comprehension.

After telling a story, give out or display an extensive list of 'personal response' questions like the one on page 86.
- These questions can be used with *any* story.
- Each student quickly chooses about five questions which they would like to respond to.

You put the students into groups of three.
- They respond to *their own* questions.
- They listen to the others responding to the questions *they* have chosen.

You remind the students that there are no 'correct' answers to these questions, and you encourage them to listen carefully to and remember their partners' ideas.
- The students can then be encouraged to write down, edit and redraft some of their responses in *written* form.
- Alternatively, they can represent their ideas as *artwork*.

The resulting writing and artwork can be made into an attractive class wall display or book.

(My thanks to Mario Rinvolucri and his inspiring work for introducing me to this simple yet brilliant idea of allowing the students to *self-select* questions from long lists – they unceasingly surprise with their imaginative responses.)

See page 86:
The Fly

Exploring ...

Your students can deepen their understanding of a story – and gain insight into their own lives and the lives of others – by exploring metaphor, imagery and the meaning of the stories you tell them.

Metaphor

Stories provide people with metaphors through which they can make sense of their own and other people's lives.
- It is useful to provide the students with a clear framework – such as a matching activity.
- This will make it easier for them to express their ideas using metaphors.

Exploration of metaphors leads to a deeper appreciation of

the significance of traditional stories across cultures.

See page 88:
The Snake Wife

Mental imagery

Students usually find it interesting to describe what they imagine when being told a story, and they learn a great deal by finding out how others have imagined the same story. They can explore and compare:

- Visual imagery – light and shade, colour, pattern, shape, foreground, background and detail.
- Auditory imagery – pitch, volume, tempo and emotion in a voice, as well as all other kinds of sounds, eg the thundering, roaring, gushing, splashing, trickling or murmuring of running water.
- Kinaesthetic imagery – type, pace, steadiness and degree of movement, as well as texture and temperature.

This type of activity can also provide the students with the tools to express themselves more creatively.

'Guided mental imagery' activities

These are suggested throughout this book. Here are some general guidelines:

- Let the students know that you are going to take them on a short journey of the imagination.
- Ask them to rest their hands on their knees and relax. Ideally, they close their eyes, but if at first they feel unsure about doing this in a teaching context, ask them to simply lower their eyes the first time you lead them through a guided imagery activity.
- Give instructions, just as you rehearsed them.
- It is a good idea to read these from a script you have prepared in advance.
- Speak more slowly, calmly and clearly than usual – and keep the language simple.
- Leave pauses between instructions, to allow time for the students to notice and remember what they imagine.
- As you come to the end, bring the students gently back to their normal awareness. Say, for example:
  When you are ready, open your eyes – and come back to the classroom.

See page 90:
After the Fire

Meaning

I find that students enjoy the opportunity to discuss the meanings in a folk tale and how these meanings relate to their own experiences and values. Rather than overtly announcing the commonly accepted meaning of a story, let them uncover their own meanings by listening closely to each other.

- They may reach a consensus about the meaning of a story.
- However, it is often interesting for both teachers and

students to realise that a story means different things to different people.

See page 92:
The Ferryman and the Grammar Teacher

Chapter Three
The student as storyteller

Storytelling ...

Students benefit enormously from building storytelling skills in a supportive learning environment. The techniques outlined here consist of step-by-step frameworks in which students can become, and then develop as, storytellers in their own right.

Repeating and retelling the story

A simple and effective way for students to learn a story is through repetition: listening to and telling the story again and again. You can use a recording of you – or someone else – telling (not reading) a short story which your students will enjoy telling outside class.

Step 1: Close listening

- Play the recording, and ask the students to listen to the voice of the storyteller.
- Play it again, making sure they understand the meaning and the vocabulary.
- Play it a third time – they should focus their attention on one or more of the following features: rhythm, pausing, word stress, intonation, linking words together, vowel sounds or consonant sounds. Which features you choose to focus on will depend on your students.

Step 2: Imitating

- Play the recording (or tell the story) once more, and stop after each phrase so that the students can repeat it – as accurately as they can.
- To get the best results, leave a few seconds' silence between the students' hearing each phrase and their saying the same phrase themselves. You can manage this by using gestures. In this silence, the students have time to 'imagine' how they are going to say it.
- Now ask them to tell the story together with the recording, 'shadowing' the voice patterns.

Step 3: Innovating

- Ask the students to sit facing each other in pairs – one will be the storyteller and the other the listener. It will work best if the more confident storyteller goes first.
- Tell them that, so far, they have been imitating the words,

intonation and stress patterns of the storyteller. Now they are ready to try telling the story their own way, using their own words.

- The listener can support the storyteller with eye contact, and prompting if necessary.
- Then they exchange roles.

Step 4: Retelling

- Encourage the students to tell the story again to different people outside class.
- Remind them that it will get better and better, and they will use their own words more and more with each telling.

If a recording is made available online, the students can be given a worksheet like the one opposite for independent learning and practice.

See page 94:
Li and Gao

Miming the story

When the students retell a story you have told them, many will try to imitate *your* model. But they should be encouraged to retell a story in their own way – by going through a process of *reinventing* the story.

- One way for them to do this is to retell the story through mimed actions – before retelling it verbally.
- As they act it out physically, they are finding their way through the story – and develop their own mental images.

They are then ready to express these images – as they retell the story, using their own words.

See page 95:
The Sleeve

Mapping the story

Most students see mental images as they listen to and tell stories. One way of remembering the events of a story is to 'map' a limited number of images as a sequence of very quick sketches, linked by arrows.

- Each student chooses which images to draw on their own piece of paper.
- They use these as visual prompts for their own retelling of the story.

The quality of the sketches is unimportant, as no-one other than the student needs to see them.

See page 96:
The Bridge

Stepping through the story

The students can learn – and remember – a story physically and collaboratively by literally 'stepping through' the story in pairs, section by section.

Repeating and retelling

- Listen to a recording of someone telling a story that you want to learn, focusing on the storyteller's voice.

- Listen again, following the meaning and checking that you understand.

- Listen again, pausing the recording after each chunk (phrase or sentence). Say it yourself and compare your pronunciation with the storyteller.

- Focus on one of the following features: rhythm, pausing, word stress, intonation, linking words together, vowel sounds or consonant sounds. Do this as many times as you like.

- Tell the story out loud, together with the recording, shadowing the storyteller's voice pattern. Do this as many times as you like.

- Tell the story to yourself, this time using your own words, as much as you like. Record yourself and then listen back, comparing your pronunciation with the storyteller. Do this as many times as you like.

- Tell the story to different people. Do this as many times as you can. Each time the story will become more and more your own.

Step 1

- Choose a short tale your students will enjoy telling, and which involves repetition.
- Tell the tale interactively with the students twice or more over a few days, so that they start to participate in the storytelling with you.

Step 2

- Make space in the classroom.
- Model how to step through the story with a confident student at your side, arms linked by the elbow if possible.
- Together, you remember and retell the story.
- When you get to the end of the first section (which would be the first paragraph if it were written down) take one step forward together.

Step 3

- Then, together with your student-partner, remember the next section – before taking another step.
- Whether you demonstrate stepping though the *whole* story or not will depend on how long it is, and on your students.
- As they watch, the other students have the chance to hear the story a second time, and fix it in their memory.

Step 4

- The students are now ready to step through the story themselves in pairs – right from the start.
- Remind them to take their time and find the detail in the story – and to be careful to avoid physical contact with the other stepping pairs!
- Each pair goes through the story at their own pace. Prompt pairs who lose track of the narrative.
- Every pair of students will step through the story in their own way:
  Some talk together, some take turns.
  Some ask and answer each other.
  Some proceed as if ticking off items on a list.
  Some mime actions.

Step 5

- When the students get to the end, bring them together and ask them what they imagined as they were stepping through the story:
  Some have mental images of the landscape of the story as they step through it.
  Some are actively involved as characters in the story.
  Some feel the temperature difference between day and night, for example, even though you may not have described this.

Step 6

- Each student can now tell the story individually to a partner, sitting face-to-face.
- A show of hands will tell you which students feel most confident to tell the story first, and these students can pair with students who prefer to go second.
- Remind the listeners to focus *supportively* on the telling, and to help the storytellers if they need prompting.
- The listeners then have their turn as storyteller.

Step 7

- Encourage the students to retell the story to someone they know outside the class. By now, they will be starting to innovate and 'make the story their own'.
- If this procedure is followed regularly – so that the students learn and retell a new story every month or so – they will become increasingly competent and confident storytellers.

You can watch young adult international learners of English following this 'stepping through the story' procedure with me on YouTube.

I came across the ideas behind this process in a wonderful workshop led by storyteller Chris Smith from The Story Museum in Oxford.
See: *www.storymuseum.org.uk/stories-at-school/frameworksandtoolkits*

See page 98:
The Silver in the Fireplace

Telling the story in character

Students find it surprisingly easy to retell a story from the perspective of one of the characters.

- This may be partly because they are not expected to remember the story *exactly* as it was told.
- There is therefore no pressure to 'get it right'.

An effective way is to create a natural 'information gap'.

- One member of the community in which the story is set knows *nothing* about the events in the story and wants to find out everything that happened from another member of the community – who was involved in the story or witnessed it all.
- The students in both roles actually know what happened, so the fun is in playing with the individual interpretations and reactions of the two 'locals'.

See page 100:
How Spider Got a Narrow Waist

Telling the story in images

Many people imagine 'moments' in a story very powerfully. You can tell your story, and then invite the students to retell it in groups – as a sequence of moments.

Step 1

Set a fixed number of 'moments', according to the story and the number of students (I recommend between six and twelve). The class agrees on the moments which they believe will tell the story well. These need to be clearly written up and displayed as a list.

Step 2

The students get into groups, and each student chooses a different moment from the list.

Step 3

They sit quietly, close their eyes and imagine their answers to the questions you will ask them.

You can adapt the following list, according to the story you have told:

- *Look at this moment in the story from a short distance away: What time of day is it? What can you see around the character or characters? What light, what shadows, what colours?*
- *Describe it – in your imagination.*
- *Now step closer, and let the picture become clearer. Look at the character or characters:
  What do you see? What about their bodies, their faces, their expressions?*
- *Move around and look at them from different positions.*
- *Can you feel the temperature at this moment in the story? Is the air still or moving? What can you smell?*
- *Choose one of the characters. Reach out and put your hand on this character's shoulder:
  How is this character feeling at this moment? What does this character want?*

- *If this moment in the story comes to life:*
  What sound can you hear?
  Where is the sound coming from?
  How does the sound make you feel?
- *Keep these ideas in your head – as you open your eyes.*

Step 4
- Ask the students to sit in pairs within their groups and to spend two minutes, each describing everything they imagined in their moment from the story.
- Ask them to edit their *two* minutes down to *one* minute, selecting the details they want to describe.
- In their group, they retell the story in order – from moment to moment – as a series of images, listening closely to each other.
- Remind them that they may have heard and imagined the story in very different ways, and to pay attention to this, but without interrupting.

Step 5
After all the students have told the story, give them time to discuss the different ways different students imagined and described the story.

Step 6
The students can individually tell the story to a partner from a different group, using any of the ideas they like from their group storytelling, as well as their own.

> See page 102:
> **Sand and Stone**

Storymaking …

Even those students who lack confidence in their ability to express themselves imaginatively find that they can create stories collaboratively – when provided with clear storymaking frameworks.

Creating the ending

The students can be invited to create and tell their own endings to an unfinished folk story – first in pairs, then as a whole class.

Step 1
Pause at a climactic point towards the end of the story and, without any preparation, invite the students to tell the ending they *imagine* to a partner:
- They might create two different endings.
- They might create one ending together.

Step 2
Invite a volunteer to sit in your storytelling seat and to tell *their* ending. The other students listen closely, and notice similarities and differences to their own endings.

Step 3
Invite another volunteer, who has a very different ending, to tell *theirs*.

Step 4
Once the students have listened to three completely different endings from other students, you could ask them to tell *their* ending again to new partner:
- They can tell their ending as before.
- They can include any ideas they liked from the other students they listened to.

Step 5
Finally, they compare their endings with the traditional ending as *you* tell it.

> See page 104:
> **The Talking Skull**

Performing the ending

The students can also create their own endings to a story by improvising in role – and then performing them.

Step 1
- In a story which involves two main characters interacting at the end, pause before you reach the ending and ask all the students, in pairs, to improvise the end of the story as a one-minute 'scene'.
- Encourage them to find voices for the two characters.
- Alternatively, you might ask the pairs to spend time scripting and rehearsing the scene.

Step 2
- Pairs then perform their endings, while the other students note similarities and differences between them.
- The above procedure can be done with students acting out the scene physically, as well as verbally, or they can concentrate on the verbal dialogue, as in a radio drama.
- In the case of a radio drama, the listeners can be asked to close their eyes during each performance.

Step 3
Finally, the students can listen to *you* telling the traditional ending to the story – and compare *their* endings.

> See page 106:
> **The Snake and the King's Dreams**

From storytelling to storymaking

Once all the main characters and the direction of the plot are sufficiently well-established, a story can be interrupted in the middle and, within the framework provided by your questioning, the students can collaboratively create their own second half of the story – not just the ending.

Step 1
- Tell the first half – until a moment of transition or suspense.

- Pause for a moment, before starting to ask (mostly open) questions.

Step 2

- After each question, wait for several students to indicate they would like to answer, before inviting just one of them to give their answer.
- Encourage as many students as possible to contribute answers as the story unfolds.
Focus on questions which move the plot along:
What happened next?
Focus on questions which stimulate mental imagery:
What did he/she see/hear/smell/feel?
- Such questions inspire creativity and aid recall when the students retell the story afterwards.
- Make sure that every contribution is incorporated by restating or, if necessary, rephrasing what the students say (see the transcript for *The Seven Parrots* on page 110).

Step 3

- Guide the storymaking, by reminding the students of unresolved narrative strands:
Remember the gold ring she was given by the angel? … What happened to that?
- Let them know what stage of the story they are at:
We're nearly at the end of the story … So what did she do after the angel took back the ring?

Step 4

- Once the story is at its end, ask pairs to immediately retell the second half of the story as they remember it. If necessary, you might do this yourself first.
- Your restating and rephrasing of students' contributions in the course of the storymaking provides a scaffold they can build on.
- However, because they have all had ownership of the storymaking, they can also add their own ideas as they retell it.

Step 5

- Finally, you tell the traditional second half of the story, and the students notice similarities and differences between the versions.
- It can be a good idea to play an extended and atmospheric piece of instrumental background music during the story *making* and *retelling* – this can guide and inspire the students and fill pauses with anticipation.
- I often play traditional music from the country where the story originates.

See page 108:
The Seven Parrots

All the stories in *Storytelling With Our Students* can be found on YouTube being told by me – just search for David Heathfield and the title of the *story*.

Also, at the time of writing, a number of videos are available of the specific *procedures* presented in the book – search for David Heathfield and title of the *activity*, to see the following:

- Facial expression (page 44)
- Interacting through personalisation (page 68)
- Predicting the story (page 71)
- From repeating to retelling (page 94)
- From miming to retelling (page 95)
- Mapping a story (page 96)
- Stepping through a story (page 98)
- Retelling a story in images (page 102)
- Creating stories (page 115)

My plan is to video more activities with my students as time goes by – in which case, there will be more for you to watch in the future. They may help you to get a more concrete sense of how the storytelling activities work.

However, I cannot over-emphasise that when *you* tell the stories, they are *your* stories, for *you* to tell *your* way.

Storytelling With Our Students has so far detailed some of the 'telling techniques' that I hope will make a big difference to your confident and successful storytelling. These techniques are briefly included alongside all the stories in the activities throughout Part B and the suggested classroom procedures.

Remember that all the techniques for storytelling overlap. Many of them are applicable much of the time, but some of them are particularly relevant to a specific story – and this will also allow you to focus on each one more specifically.

But first, before you tell *any* story, decide how you might open the story – to capture your students' full attention and achieve the storytelling atmosphere you would like to create.

And then, of course, you need to choose how you will close the story.

Opening

The opening of a story sends an important signal to the listeners – a 'transition' between the world of the classroom and the world of the story.

- You might say:
  Once upon a time …
  Long, long ago …
  or
  There was once …
- You might start with a sound, a song or a piece of music.
- You might show a picture, reveal an object or do a mime.

There are so many openings available – we can make up our own, or we can borrow them from different languages and cultures.

Below are just a few of my favourites – in storyteller Sam Canarozzi's fabulous collection of openings and endings from around the world: *When Tigers Smoked Pipes* (Society for Storytelling Press 2008).

- Arabic:
  Kan ma kan, fiqadim azzaman …
  It was, it was not, in the old, old times …

- Japanese:
  Mukashi, mukashi …
  Very, very long ago …

- Polish:

  Dawno, dawno temu, za siedmioma górami, za siedmioma lasami i za siedmioma rzekami …

  Once upon a time, beyond the seven mountains, beyond the seven forests, beyond the seven rivers …

In Caribbean storytelling, there is often a 'call and response' opening:

The teller calls **Cric!**

The listeners respond **Crac!**

- They do this three times in succession, each time more loudly than before – building the level of energy to launch into the story *telling* and story *listening*.
- The storyteller makes use of this Cric-Crac 'call and response' at any point during the story, to make sure the listeners are paying full attention.

Another Caribbean opening is:

Storyteller: *How many ears do you have?*

Listeners: *Two!*

Storyteller: *Then find yourselves a third one and listen to what I say!*

'Call and response' is common in African storytelling, too: See *Mbongoro* on page 84.

Closing

Of course, the closing is equally important – it is a good idea to rehearse this, too, so that you make an impact with your ending. As with the opening, a song, a piece of music, a picture or an object can all be effective.

Below are translations of a few of the many story endings collected by Sam Canarozzi.

Saudi Arabia:

My story did I tell, in your heart let it swell.

Northern Angola:

And now that my story's done, I throw it back into the fire.

Melanesia:

And so they left us a great heap of stories. And it was one of those that I gave you tonight.

Germany:

And if they aren't dead, they're living still.

Norway:

And my story happened east of the sun and west of the moon.

Lebanon:

We were really there in the story, but we're back now.

Brittany, France:

This story happened when chickens had teeth. The teeth fell out, but the story remains.

And perhaps my favourite ending of all is from Albania:

And three apples fell from a tree:
The first apple is for the one who told the story.
The second for the one who listened.
And the last apple for the one who will tell the story to others.

See also the delightful 'Shortest Tale' on page 126.

● ● ●

This now brings us to how you can first rehearse, and then use to maximum effect, your most important storytelling 'instrument' – your own voice.

Chapter One

The teacher as storyteller

'The power of storytelling lies in the fact that the teacher is in direct communication with the class, she is not dealing with 'third person' text, by telling a story she makes it her own.'

Mario Rinvolucri
Teacher, teacher trainer and author

Technique	Story	Page
Using your voice	*The Story of Sidwell*	40
Giving the characters voices	*The Dog and the Wolf*	42
Facial expression	*The Village of Fools*	44
Movement and gesture	*Ngaardi and Toonkoo*	45
Mimed actions	*Manju*	46
Accompanying the story	*Filling the House*	48
Repetition of words	*Maui and the Great Fish*	50
Repetition of phrases	*Anansi and Tiger*	52
Repetition of phrases with alterations	*Lazy Jack*	54
Repetition of rhymes	*Juan and the Magic Tree*	56
Repetition of episodes	*The Witch of Tavistock*	58
Interacting with the characters	*Bedd Gelert*	60
Interacting with the students	*How to Weigh an Elephant*	62
Interacting through interruptions	*Cloud Eating*	63
Interacting through riddles	*A Question of Brains*	64
Interacting through different cultures	*The Three Golden Hairs* *Jackal and the Shining Child*	66
Interacting through personalisation	*The Lost Axe*	68

Using your voice

A telling technique

By subtly modulating the pitch, tempo and volume of your voice as you tell a story, you can convey such things as emotion, attitude, action and mystery.

The Story of Sidwell is from my home city of Exeter in the South West of England, and dates back one and a half thousand years to the end of the Roman rule and the beginnings of Christianity. The story was written down in Latin over a thousand years ago. St Sidwell's church has now become a wonderful community centre supporting marginalised groups in Exeter, so it's definitely the right story for me to start with.

To rehearse telling this tale, pay particular attention to how you use your voice. Try out these suggestions and find out if they work for you:

- Tell the first part of the story evenly, with little variation in pitch, volume and tempo – so that it will be noticeable when you *do* alter your voice later.
- When the mower hesitates before killing Sidwell, pause a moment and then continue with increased volume and tempo until he has run away.
- Slow down the tempo – and lower the volume and pitch of your voice – as you describe the wonder of Sidwell walking towards the East Gate during the night and the miracle of the holy water.

Before telling

Tell the students that you are going to tell them a legend from the old English city of Exeter, which was written down in Latin more than a thousand years ago.

While telling

Use your voice as when you were rehearsing, but be ready to modify the way you tell the story in response to what happens as you tell it. Remember that storytelling is co-creative and that, every time, you need to fit the story to the listeners in front of you.

After telling

Slow down the tempo, and soften the tone of your voice still further – as you lead the students through this guided 'mental imagery' activity.

Say: *Close your eyes and sit quietly. While you were listening to The Story of Sidwell, you may have experienced different feelings at different moments.*

- *Remember one moment where you had negative feelings about a character in the story …*
- *How do you feel about that character at that moment? Why do you feel that way? What do you want that character to do? What should happen to that character? …*
- *Now remember one moment where you had positive feelings about a character …*
- *How do you feel about that character at that moment? Why do you feel that way?*

Now slowly come back to this room. You can open your eyes and sit still.'

Gently interview a volunteer student who would like to describe both their negative and positive moments and feelings in front of the class.

Increase the tempo, pitch and volume of your voice – you are now returning to 'classroom management' mode.

- Find out which other students would like to describe one or both of *their* moments. They can do this in pairs.
- If some students prefer not to, invite them to join a pair – and to listen and ask questions.

Once the pairs or groups of three have finished, find out from the whole class which moments were chosen, and allow time for the students to comment on what they felt.

Stories are emotional journeys for listeners, so manage activities like this one with sensitivity.

To follow on, tell the students that – although there is no reference in the written account to her being a Christian – Sidwell was made the Patron Saint of Exeter.

- There are stories of martyrs in many faiths and cultures: some are legends, while others are verified historical accounts.
- The students can research and each prepare to tell the legend of a different martyr.

The Story of Sidwell

A legend from Devon, England

Long ago, when Exeter was still a young city, there lived a rich man called Beorna.

He owned the land beyond the East Gate of the city, and he employed a mower to cut the long grass that grew there.

Beorna had a daughter called Sidwell. She was good and kind and bold and everyone loved her, except for her stepmother whose heart was full of jealousy.

One day, the jealous stepmother came out of the East Gate and up to the mower who was cutting the long grass with his sharp scythe. She said:

'You are a poor man, though you work hard. I can make you rich. Tomorrow, Sidwell will bring you food. If you kill her, I will fill your hands with gold.'

The next day, the East Gate opened and Sidwell stepped towards the mower. Her face shone with an inner beauty, and she held out a bowl of food to the hardworking mower.

The poor man stopped working and looked at her. He saw her goodness and her kindness and his heart was full of sorrow.

But he remembered the gold.

He lifted the sharp scythe high and, with a single stroke, he cut off her head.

He looked down at her body where she fell, and the blood spattered on the ground.

He forgot the gold and dropped the scythe. He ran as fast as he could to the East, and never returned.

That night, the watchmen at the East Gate saw the heavens open, and a bright beam of light shone down on the long grass where the girl had died.

The next night, the beam of light shone down in the same place.

On the third night, the citizens of Exeter gathered at the East Gate to look where the watchmen had told them.

Among the citizens were the stepmother and Beorna himself, who missed his daughter and wondered where she was.

Suddenly the heavens opened, and the bright beam of light shone down on the long grass.

Sidwell rose to her feet and stepped slowly towards the East Gate. Under one arm she held her own head, and in the other hand she held the sharp scythe. Outside the East gate, she lay down in the long grass.

The people of Exeter were frightened. In the morning, at first light, they opened the East Gate and came to that place.

They found Sidwell, beautiful and dead, her head once more fixed upon her shoulders.

There, they prepared to build a tomb.

Later, they found the place where she was killed. A spring of pure water gushed forth from the ground.

These were healing waters.

Those who were ill drank the water and became well. The blind could see and the lame could walk.

This was a holy well.

In the place where her body lay, a church was built in her name, the Church of St Sidwell, and there it still stands.

Saint Sidwell is the patron saint of Exeter, one of the oldest cities in England.

Giving the characters voices

A telling technique

Finding different voices for different characters adds variety to your storytelling, and has an impact on your listeners.

The Dog and the Wolf was given to me by my friend Serhiy Vasilyev, who has done more storytelling with me than any other student. I have since told this popular Ukrainian and Russian tale of friendship to hundreds of students.

To rehearse, find distinct voices for the characters in the story. The hungry wolf talks in rhyme, so try giving him a more exaggerated voice than the one you give the farmer.

- A deep, slow, growling voice with the authority and certainty of a top predator is the wolf voice that works for me – in combination with an 'about to pounce' posture.
- You might spend time trying out different voices for the characters before you find the ones for *you*, or they might come straight away.

Commit yourself to the voices you choose – if *you* do them with conviction, the *students* will be convinced.

Before telling

Ask the students if they have dogs:
Are they 'working' dogs? How old are they?
Discuss what should be done with old working dogs, once they can no longer do their job. Perhaps dedicate the story to one of the students' dogs.

While telling

Use the character voices that you rehearsed. You could encourage the students to join in:
- They bark when the dog barks.
- They howl when the wolf howls.

After telling

Ask the students to describe, and/or draw, the dog, the wolf, the villagers, the farm, the forest – as they imagine them. If you can, show some or all of the ten-minute award-winning animation of this tale: the students compare their mental images with the way the same images are portrayed in the cartoon. Just search on YouTube for 'There once was a dog by Eduard Nazarov'.

To follow on, explain that people tend to mix socially with others from similar backgrounds and with similar lifestyles.
- Dog and wolf help each other, but have little in common.
- Have the students ever helped or been helped by someone from a different background with a different lifestyle?

The Dog and the Wolf
A story from Ukraine

Sirko was an old dog. No longer could he see well; his hearing was weak and he was too slow to catch the rats on the farm.

The farmer said, 'I feed you but you're of no use to me anymore,' and he drove Sirko away from the farm, across the fields and into the forest.

As it grew dark, Sirko made his way between the trees. He had never been alone. He had never had to find food for himself. He had always been fed by the hand of his master, the farmer.

Soon he could see nothing, and the sounds of the forest troubled the old dog.

He caught the scent of a creature coming closer, a strange scent, different from any he had smelt before, and yet it was familiar.

Suddenly he was standing snout to snout with a creature bigger than himself, a long-legged, lean, hungry, wild wolf:
'Now why a creature tame and mild
Should make his way into my wild?'

Sirko said all that had happened, and the wild wolf listened closely:
'If you drive me from the farm,
They'll welcome you back with open arms.'

That night, Sirko stayed with the wild wolf under the cover of the forest and, at first light, the two creatures made their way through the trees and across the fields towards the farm.

Sirko hid behind the farmyard wall, while the wolf jumped over the gate and padded silently across the farmyard towards the back door of the farmhouse, where the farmer's wife had put their new-born baby in a cradle outside to breathe the morning air.

The wolf took the baby between his sharp teeth, turned, ran, and leapt over the farmyard gate and made off across the fields towards the forest.

Sirko jumped out from behind the wall and gave chase, barking as loud as an old dog can.

The famer and his wife came running out of the house, only to see the wolf running off with their baby.

But now there was Sirko running after the wolf, jumping onto the wolf's back. There was a cloud of dust as the dog and the wolf fought, flashes of teeth and claws.

The Dog and the Wolf

The farmer and his wife ran as fast as they could.

But now the wolf was yelping and running towards the trees, and Sirko was carrying the baby carefully back towards the farm.

The farmer's wife took and held her baby, and tears of joy ran down her cheeks. The farmer took the old dog in his arms:
'Sirko, how could I ever have driven you away? You saved our child from the wolf. You are a hero. Tonight there will be a great feast in your honour.'

All day long, Sirko thought only of how his friend, the hungry wolf, had helped him.

As the light faded, Sirko made his way across the fields and into the forest to look for the wolf and invite him to the feast as his guest of honour.

In the darkness, the shadows of two creatures, the dog and the wolf, crossed the fields to the farmyard. The old dog climbed under the gate, the hungry wolf jumped over the gate and, together, they entered the stone barn where the feast would take place.

As yet, no one was there.

Sirko hid the wolf under the long table and waited.

Soon the villagers began to arrive, carrying dishes of food: roast meats, sausages, borscht and bread.

When the feasting began, Sirko brought food under the long table, and the wolf began to fill his belly.

More and more roast meat and sausages Sirko took from the table, and more and more roast meat and sausages disappeared down the wolf's throat.

The people drank vodka and sang a drinking song, their voices loud and clear.

The wolf stopped eating and listened:
'My belly has stopped rumbling,
I've had enough, now I will sing.'

'No!' cried Sirko, 'You are a wolf. They will kill you. I will bring you more roast meat and sausages.'

The farmers' neighbours said, 'Your old dog is eating too much. You should beat him.'

'My old dog saved my child from the wolf. My old dog is a hero. Sirko, take all the meat you want.'

The wolf was no longer lean. The wolf was no longer hungry. The grease dripped from his lips.

Once more the people sang, this time louder than before.

Under the long table, the wolf again stopped and listened:
'Now I've eaten everything,
It is my turn, now I will sing.'

And before Sirko could stop him, the wolf lifted his snout under the long table, shut his eyes tight – and sang.

A long howl filled the barn.

The villagers fell silent and stood up, fear in their eyes.

They picked up their meat knives and kicked over the long table. There was the fat and greasy wolf, eyes tight shut, howling long and loud.

They stepped towards the wolf, their knives raised.

What could Sirko do to save his friend wolf?

He took the end of the wolf's tail between his teeth and bit down as hard as he could.

The wolf's eyes sprang open and he saw the knives. The heavy wolf ran for the barn door and out into the farmyard.

Sirko was after him, barking as loudly as an old dog can. The fat wolf just managed to jump over the gate.

Sirko shot under the gate and chased the yelping wolf across the fields and into the blackness of the forest, as the villagers stood in the farmyard and listened.

There among the trees, the two friends stood panting, snout to snout. The old dog knew he would never see his friend wolf again.

The wolf's eyes glinted in the darkness:
'Your world is tame, your world is mild,
I choose hunger, I choose wild.'

Sirko returned once more to a hero's welcome. He had saved the village from the wolf twice in one day.

The rest of his life, he lived in the comfort of the farmer's family, well fed and looked after, as all old dogs should be.

But he never forgot the wolf and, every now and then when the moon was full and high, the old dog listened at the farmyard gate.

Although his hearing was weak, he could just make out the sound of the lean and hungry wild wolf, singing.

Facial expression

A telling technique

Your face becomes more animated than usual when you tell a story, and your expression can transform the meaning of your words – whether you are speaking as the narrator or as a character.

The Village of Fools is a marvellously silly and simple tale told to me by Finnish teacher Merja Nykänen.

To rehearse, be conscious of what your face is doing – and play with exaggerating your expressions, particularly when you become 'the village of fools'.

- As you start the story – *There was once a village of fools* – smile slightly, raise your eyebrows and nod knowingly at your students, so that they start anticipating what might happen in the story.
- When you start speaking the words of the foolish *women*, make an exaggerated *grinning* face – a foolish voice will follow automatically.
- When you start speaking as the foolish *men*, make a totally different exaggerated *surprised* face – a very different foolish voice will come out.
- As soon as you become narrator again, drop the exaggerated expression and voice.
- Matti's expression is more subtle – as you speak his words, you may express gentle amusement or mild irritation.

Before telling

Ask the students to close their eyes and imagine being in a house without windows, then to keep their eyes closed while they listen to you describe a favourite window – the view, the design, the light – and perhaps a little personal anecdote.

Ask them to describe *their* favourite window to a partner.

While telling

Use your exaggerated facial expressions and matching voices.

After telling

Ask the students to stand facing each other in pairs. Say:

- *You are two villagers and you have just finished your first window. One of you is looking out and the other is looking in. Show how foolish and excited you are – using your eyes, eyebrows, mouth, head …*
- *Talk through the window. Keep your expressions and let your voice follow. Talk about your wonderful window, how you feel, what you are going to do …*
  3–2–1 Action!

Some pairs can perform for the rest of the class – you might need to tell the others not to laugh too loud! How did they feel doing this activity? Playing the fool is often a liberating experience in a learning situation.

To follow on, ask the students to prepare to tell a 'fool tale' for the next class – they are found in all cultures. They can go to *www.pitt.edu*, search for folk texts and look under F.

The Village of Fools

A tale from Finland

There was once a village of fools.

One day, Matti the wise man walked into the village.

The people were pleased with themselves because they had built a house to live in.

Matti found the women holding bags wide open, then closing their bags and running into the house.

'What are you doing?' asked Matti.
The women answered:
'Matti, Matti, we're catching the light outside and carrying it inside. It's not hard work, because the light is not heavy. We're running as fast as we can, but it's still so dark in the house.'

Matti found the men running out of the door of the house with closed bags, and then opening their bags wide and shaking them.

'What are you doing?' asked Matti.
The men answered:
'Matti, Matti, we're catching the darkness inside and carrying it outside. It's not hard work, because the darkness is not heavy. We're running as fast as we can, but it's still so dark in the house.'

'Then I will tell you all how to make a window, so the light comes in.'

Matti told them how to make a window, then departed.

Next time Matti walked into the village, he found the fools. But where was the house?

'Matti, Matti, we made a window and some light came in. So we made another window, and some more light came in. So we made more windows, and the light was good. So we made more windows and more windows – and then the house fell down.'

Matti looked at the fools and shook his head.
Then Matti went on his way.

The villagers were sorry about the house, then one of them said: 'It's not so bad. Now we have so much light!'

Movement and gesture

A telling technique

Storytelling involves as much non-verbal as verbal communication, so it is crucial to be conscious of movement and gesture, as well as facial expression, however big or small.

Ngaardi and Toonkoo is a lovely South Eastern Australian aboriginal creation myth I first found in a beautifully illustrated children's book.

To rehearse, try out some different movements and gestures. Practise them, so that they begin to come naturally. Here are some suggestions to experiment with:

- Tell the first part of the story seated, and track the trajectory of the shooting star with a raised hand.
- Look up and gaze longingly at a fixed point when you describe Ngaardi looking up at the moon and seeing Toonkoo.
- Stand up when you describe Ngaardi leaving the fire, and remain on your feet to the end.
- Sigh softly as you describe Ngaardi's sigh which brings Creation.
- Look down at the end, and imagine the waratah flower growing just in front of you.

However, be sparing – so your movements *support* the narrative, rather than *take it over*.

Before telling

Point out that this is a story which explains Creation and is sacred even today to some Australian aboriginal people.

While telling

Be confident – and support your words with strongly defined movements, gestures and expressions, just as you rehearsed.

After telling

Elicit that this story explains the mythological origin of the boomerang, the appearance of the moon, the first water, the light of Creation and the waratah flower.

Ask the students to talk in small groups and find similarities in this creation story to stories they know from their own and other cultures. These similarities can then be discussed as a whole class.

To follow on, the students can look for more folk tales about the moon. They can listen to me telling *Rabbit and Jaguar* – a wonderful Mayan story – on the fantastic World Stories website, and read the transcript: *www.worldstories.org.uk/ stories/story/37-the-rabbit-and-the-jaguar/english*. (See also page 113 – for a 'bilingual' procedure for telling this tale.)

Ngaardi and Toonkoo

A creation myth from Australia

The first man and the first woman came to the world, riding on a shooting star.

The first woman, Ngaardi, gathered herbs, dug roots from the ground and made fire. There she cooked and told stories to the children, and the kookaburra laughed.

The first man, Toonkoo, took his spear and went hunting, guided by Darama, the Great Spirit.

Every time Toonkoo looked up, there was Darama watching him. After some time, Toonkoo became angry. He threw his spear up at Darama, but the Great Spirit caught the spear and bent it and threw it back down.

This was the first boomerang.

Darama took Toonkoo and put him in the Moon.

Ngaardi sat by the fire and waited for Toonkoo, but he did not return.

She looked up, and saw Toonkoo in the Moon.

She reached up, but she could not touch him.

She left the fire and began to climb the highest mountain. She climbed and climbed until she was at the top.

Again she looked up and saw Toonkoo in the Moon.

She reached up, but she could not touch him.

The tears ran down her cheeks and down the mountain, forming the first rivers and the first waterholes.

She sighed, and with her sigh came the dawn of Creation.

She lay down and left her heart there at the top of the mountain so that Toonkoo would find it if he ever came back.

Her heart is the red flower called Waratah.

Mimed actions

A telling technique

A story told with mime is not only entertaining but also easy for students to join in with – both physically and verbally.

Manju is a Japanese folk tale from the humorous Rakugo tradition. It was told in one of my classes by a wonderfully exuberant student storyteller, Satomi Endo.

To rehearse, be ready to tell your students about something you are afraid of – the more irrational the fear the better. Practise all the different mimed actions you are going to do while telling the story.

Before telling

Say: *I'm afraid of …*, and tell the students one or two short anecdotes related to this fear. In my case, I am less afraid of spiders than I was a few years ago but, even now, there's no way I could hold a big one in my hand.

While telling

Do a different mimed action for each of the six creatures that the first six friends are afraid of:

- When you mime the actions, it is enough to just use your fingers, hands and arms.
- Express fear in your voice for each of them.
- Invite the students to join in with the mimed actions, which can serve as prompts for them to recall and say the creatures along with you – the second time around.

You can also do mimed actions for what Mr Pine says he'll do with each of these creatures.

It is a good idea to stop at the point where the friends decide on a plan, and to invite the students to guess the ending of the story in pairs and then exchange their ideas with other pairs.

After telling

Invite the students to ask each other about the creatures in the story:
Are you/Aren't you afraid of …?
And to ask each other:
What are you afraid of?

To follow on, include the discussion of students' fears into new retellings of the story:

- Incorporate the six most irrational fears the students in the class have admitted to.
- Replace Mr Pine's name with the name of a particularly fearless or resourceful student.

Groups of three can create their own version, and then the groups split up, forming new groups of three to tell each other their stories.

Manju

A Japanese folk tale

Seven friends were talking about what they were afraid of.

'I'm afraid of snakes, they move in zigzags.'
'I'm afraid of foxes, they turn into ghosts.'
'I'm afraid of bats, they fly at night.'
'I'm afraid of spiders, they make sticky webs.'
'I'm afraid of caterpillars, they hide under leaves.'
'I'm afraid of ants, they travel in long trails.'

'Mr Pine, what are you afraid of?'

Mr Pine lay on the tatami mat, resting this head
in his hand.
'I'm afraid of nothing.'

'Aren't you afraid of snakes?'
'If I find a snake, I'll wrap it around my head to keep me
warm.'

'Aren't you afraid of foxes?'
'If I find a fox and it turns into a ghost, I'll make it into
my slave.'

'Aren't you afraid of bats?'
'If I catch a bat, I'll make it into an umbrella.'

'Aren't you afraid of spiders?'
'If I find a spider, I'll use its web to make sticky natto
and I'll add the spider for flavour.'

'Aren't you afraid of caterpillars?'
'If I find a caterpillar, I'll tie it to a stick and use it as a
toothbrush.'

'Aren't you afraid of ants?'
'If I find ants, I'll take a handful and sprinkle them
over my rice instead of sesame.'

'But Mr Pine, you must be afraid of something. Everyone
is afraid of something. What are you afraid of?'

'I'm afraid of … Oh, I'm so afraid of … MANJU!'

'Mr Pine, what kind of creature is manju?'
'Manju is not a creature. Manju are sticky buns with
fillings. I'm very afraid!'

Mr Pine opened the paper screen door to the bedroom
and closed it behind him. He lay down on the futon bed
and hid under the covers, shaking with fear.

His friends looked at each other. They secretly made a
plan.

They went to the manju store. They bought buckwheat
manju, chestnut manju, sake manju, red and white
manju, hot manju, sweet manju …

What other kinds of manju?

They carried the manju on a tray, opened the paper
screen door, crept into the bedroom, put down the tray
next to the futon where Mr Pine was hiding under the
covers, crept out of the bedroom, slid the paper screen
door closed – and waited …

'Oh oh oh manju, oh, I'm afraid. Oh buckwheat manju,
oh chestnut manju … mmm very tasty; oh sake manju …
delicious; oh my favourite … red and white manju;
mmm … hot manju; aaah sweet manju …'

The friends rushed into the room, to find Mr Pine finishing
the last manju.

'Mr Pine … Aren't you afraid of manju?'
'Oh no, I forgot … I love manju.'

'But Mr Pine, what are you afraid of?'
'I'm afraid of … a nice cup of Japanese green tea!'

Accompanying the story

A telling technique

Accompanying your storytelling – with live music, song, percussion and sound effects – offers you and your students wide-ranging opportunities for creative expression.

Filling the House is a riddle tale with many variant forms. Irish American storyteller Patrick Ryan was the first person I heard tell a similar version to this one.

To rehearse, get a piece of rhythmic and celebratory music ready – to be played as you tell the end of the story.
- You can prepare a piece of suitable recorded music (here, perhaps an Irish jig played on a solo fiddle – such as on YouTube: *www.youtube.com/watch?v=7G7Uy0XlJwE*).
- Alternatively, hide a musical instrument in the classroom – to be played by you or by a student (who you would probably need to tell in advance and swear to secrecy, unless you know the student loves improvising).

Before telling

Let the students know that the story they are about to hear involves a problem that needs solving.

While telling

As with all problem-solving tales, the listeners are likely to start guessing the solution as the story unfolds.

They will pick up that the youngest son is bound to solve it – it is a 'pattern of three' story – so when it gets to Jack's turn, pause and invite the students to talk in pairs and come up with solutions.
- The students listen to all of the solutions the class have come up with.
- They vote for the one they think is the most likely for Jack in the story.

(This problem appears in folk tales in many different cultures and, in many of these tales, a candle is lit – filling the room with light – so some students may be surprised that this is not the solution in *this* story.)

Now tell the end of the story.

When the music begins, get the students to clap their hands and tap their feet in time with the rhythm – to build the energy and create an atmosphere of celebration.

After telling

Prepare the students to share personal stories about the role of music in their lives. To launch the discussion, read aloud the following questions and ask the students to briefly note their answers on paper:
- *What was the first time you remember hearing music as a child?*
  Where were you?
  Who were you with?
  What was the music?
- *Which piece of music brings back a memory whenever you hear it?*
  What memory?
  What feelings?
- *Which musical performance is memorable for you?*
  Were you playing, singing, dancing – or listening?
  Why do you remember it so well?

In groups of three, the students share their personal stories, choosing the questions they want to answer.

Finally, hold a discussion with the whole class about the role of music in people's lives, bearing in mind that, for some students, music will be far more central to their identity than for others.

To follow on, you can make this story into a lead-in to the topic of music.
- The students can prepare short talks on music.
- They may play a favourite track.
- They may play a recording of themselves in concert.
- They may even perform live for their peers.

Filling the House

A tale from Ireland

Once, there lived an old farmer with three sons. He called them to his bed and said:

'Soon I will die, and one of you will have the farm. Whichever one of you can fill the house from top to bottom and from corner to corner with one thing, he will have the farm.'

Well, the farmhouse was small and the eldest son jumped up:
'I can fill the house!'

He ran to the stable to fetch the old carthorse and led it to the house. The great horse had to bend its head low to get through the front door, and there it stood. Its nose touched one wall and its tail flicked at the opposite wall. Its ears tickled the rafters in the roof.

'I've filled the house with the horse,' called the eldest son.

The old farmer climbed out of his bed and stood before the horse. He held his hands above the horse's back and below the horse's belly.
'There's space around the horse. The house is not quite full.'

And he got back into bed.

The second son jumped up:
'I can fill the house!'

He led the horse back out through the front door and to the barn. There, he harnessed the horse to the cart. He reached for the pitchfork and began to put hay into the cart. He worked hard filling the cart, and then led the horse and cart to the front door of the farmhouse.

He pitched the hay into the house until the hay filled the house from top to bottom and from corner to corner.

'I've filled the house with hay,' called the second son.

The old farmer climbed out of his bed and found he could see nothing because there was hay all around him. He held his hands out to his sides. The hay reached from wall to wall. He reached out above his head and stretched his fingers to the rafters in the roof.

The hay had begun to settle.
'There's a little space between the hay and the roof. The house is not quite full.'

And he got back into bed.

The two older sons emptied the house of hay, took the horse back to the stable and came and sat once more beside their father's bed.

The youngest son was called Jack, and everyone thought him a fool. Now Jack looked around at his brothers' unhappy faces and did what he always did when they needed cheering up.

He got up and went to the corner and picked up a black leather case. He opened the case, took out his fiddle and began to play a sweet melody.

Soon, smiles appeared on his brothers' faces, and they began to tap their feet to the rhythm of the music.

The old farmer sat up in bed and began to hum along.

The door opened, and in came the women and soon there was dancing. The old farmer called out:

'Jack, you have filled the house from top to bottom and from corner to corner. You have filled the house with music. And your music has filled the house with joy, with laughter and with love.'

Jack just smiled, and carried on playing his merry tune. He had no plan to keep the farm for himself.

After all, what was music, or any other thing, if it wasn't for sharing?

Repetition of words

A telling technique

Choral repetition is a feature of oral storytelling around the world. Rhythmically repeating three times the same key action verb – chorally with the students – at two or more points during a story is easy for them to join in with, especially when accompanied by mime or gesture.

Maui and the Great Fish is my retelling of part of the Maori creation myth New Zealanders all grow up with. The Maori people arrived in New Zealand from Eastern Polynesia before the 13th century and developed a sophisticated culture.

To rehearse this tale, focus on matching the rhythm of the repeated verb phrase *'they paddled and they paddled and they paddled'* with a clearly-mimed paddling action.
- There should be exactly the same emphatic rhythm every time, making it fun and easy for the students to repeat along with you.
- In order for the students to join in, it is usually necessary to invite them with a smile, a moment's pause and an open-handed gesture.

Be ready to use plenty of mimed actions, and find a distinct voice for Maui, the trickster with superpowers.

Before telling

Ask the students who has a younger brother or sister and what they find annoying about them. Also, find out:
- Who *is* a youngest brother or sister? How do *they* annoy *their* older brothers or sisters?
- What do they know about New Zealand?
- What powers might a hero in a story have – fly, lift incredible weights, become invisible … ?

While telling

Tell this creation myth in a fun and lively way.

After telling

Give each student thirty seconds to listen closely to one other student commenting on one thing about the story that made an impression on them. They then summarise back to the other student what they said – in *one* sentence – in order to check the main idea.

Now invite volunteer students to say their summary sentences about what made an impression on their partner. For example:

'When Maui was making the waves get bigger, it reminded Yan of when he was on a ferry crossing during a storm near his home town.'

Challenge the students to remember the repeated words and phrases in the story. If they – and you – do the mimed actions, they will recall them more easily.

Ask what *kind* of tale this is.

- Discuss the fact that there are creation myths in all cultures which explain the beginning of the world: how natural features of the landscape, creatures and plants came to be the way they are.
- Ask the students to remember – or find – a short creation myth from any culture, and to prepare to tell it in the following lesson.

To follow on, get the students to do the same mimed paddling action the following day, and find out if they can still remember the repeated phrases:

'They paddled and they paddled and they paddled.'
'I am with you. You can't you see me.'

They then exchange *their* creation myths in small groups.

Maui and the Great Fish

A creation myth from New Zealand

Does your younger brother or younger sister ever get on your nerves? Do you ever get on your older brother or older sister's nerves?

Maui was the youngest of all the sons of the Sky God. He had great powers, but his older brothers were tired of his constant tricks. They wanted to get away from him, so they got up early before dawn to go fishing in their canoe.

Far out across the calm clear sea they paddled and they paddled and they paddled.

They took up their spears and were about to start fishing, when they heard a voice:
'I am with you. You can't see me.'

The brothers were afraid. They looked around but there was nothing on the horizon.
Where was the strange voice coming from?
Further out across the calm clear sea they paddled and they paddled and they paddled.

Again they took up their spears and were about to start fishing, when they heard the voice:
'I am with you. You can't see me.'

The brothers were frightened. They looked over the edge of the canoe, but the water below was clear and empty.
Where was the strange voice coming from?
Still further out across the calm, clear sea they paddled and they paddled and they paddled.

They took up their spears and were about to start fishing, when they heard:
'I am with you. You can't see me.'

The brothers were terrified. They looked up into the sky which was clear and empty.
Where was the strange voice coming from?
They were just about to start paddling again, when the eldest brother reached down and pulled up the footboard in the bottom of the canoe.

Hiding beneath was Maui, their youngest brother.
'I was with you. You couldn't see me!'

Maui's brothers were angry.
'We're taking you straight back to shore!'

'But look how far away the shore is!' said Maui, pointing. It was a tiny speck in the distance. Maui had the power to make things seem much further away than they were.

The brothers took up their spears and were about to start fishing, but Maui said:
'There are no fish here, just paddle a little further.'

The brothers knew about Maui's powers, so they paddled and they paddled and they paddled, until Maui told them to stop.
'Here there are fish. We'll catch plenty here.'

'We'll catch the fish without you, Maui. You'll wait.'

Maui's brothers soon filled the canoe with beautiful large fish.
'Now we'll paddle back to shore.'

Maui took out his magic fish hook, made from his ancestor's jawbone, and tied it to a line.
'It's my turn to fish now. Give me some bait.'

Maui's brothers turned their backs, so Maui began to rub his nose. He rubbed until his nose began to bleed.

He smeared the blood onto the hook and dropped it over the side, letting the line out so the hook sank deeper and deeper into the sea until, finally, Maui had a catch.

He pulled hard on the line: 'Help me, brothers!'
But the brothers kept their backs turned. Maui summoned up all his power and pulled on the line.

The sea began to rise and churn.

Maui pulled harder, and great waves rose and crashed over the canoe. Maui's brothers held on to the sides, frightened for their lives.

Maui pulled, until a great fish, smooth-skinned and as wide as the sea itself, rose above the surface.

'What have I done? I have pulled up the Sea God from the bottom of the sea. I must go to tell our father, the Sky God. Brothers, leave this smooth-skinned fish alone.'

Maui flew off into the sky to find his father.

As soon as he had gone, his brothers began to fight over the fish.

They took up their spears and slashed at the fish, each claiming his own part.

When Maui returned, the skin of the great fish was no longer smooth. There were high mountains and deep valleys.

This fish remains and is today called New Zealand.

Repetition of phrases

A telling technique

Repeating a phrase while being told a story not only helps students remember the form and meaning of the phrase but also – by saying it with you – they internalise the speech pattern and pronunciation.

Anansi and Tiger is one of a huge number of popular Anansi tales which people brought with them across the Atlantic from West Africa to the Caribbean during the slave trade. Kwaku Anansi, as he is called in Ghana, is a trickster who appears both in the form of man and spider.

To rehearse, imagine the students in front of you and how you will get them to join in. In this tale, the phrase *'Oh Beautiful Tiger, Magnificent Tiger, just one thing I ask'* is repeated several times, so it will be easy for the students to join in with it.

Before telling

Say to the whole class they are going to act out a scene: *Stand in pairs. You are A and B.*
* *A is playing a new game and B has never played this game and really wants to try it. B has nothing to offer A in exchange for trying the game – so the only thing B can do is to flatter A.*
* *B can compliment A on everything: personality, clothes, hair, studies, sports, friends – and anything else. What B really wants is to try A's new game.*
* *A is going to enjoy all this flattery and, in the end – if B is successful – A is going to let B try the new game.*
OK …
A: Let's see you playing your new game.
B: Get ready to start flattering A.
Ready?
3–2–1 Action!

When they have finished, invite the students to listen to you telling this Jamaican/West African story about Anansi the Trickster.

While telling

* The first time you come to the phrase to be repeated – *'Oh Beautiful Tiger, Magnificent Tiger, just one thing I ask'* – pause momentarily and lean forward, before saying it with added emphasis.
* The second time, slow down your speech tempo just beforehand, and gesture with open hands to invite the students to say the phrase along with you – but be careful not to lose the rhythm of the story.

As you go on, the students will join in more confidently with the repeated phrase – perhaps so much so that, by the last time, you can be quiet and let *them* say the repeated phrase in your place.

After telling

Ask the pairs to compare Anansi's story with the scene they created before listening.

Say: *A and B, you are going to do your scene again – in one minute. This time, you might use some of the flattery techniques that Anansi used. Make sure that B gets to play the game in the end. Afterwards, you can show your scene to other students. Get ready.*
3–2–1 Action!

Find out from the whole class if the strategies they used were similar to Anansi's flattery of Tiger.

Invite one or two volunteer pairs to show their one-minute scene to the whole class, and invite comments from the other students about the strategies they use. Then ask each pair to join another pair, and to show each other their scenes – and comment.

As a class, get the students to discuss the common sayings in English *'Flattery will get you everywhere'* and *'Flattery will get you nowhere'*.
* Can they give specific examples from their own experience to support their arguments about which one they believe is more true?
* Are there similar sayings in other languages the students know?

To follow on, ask pairs or small groups of students to first improvise and then perform sketches illustrating examples from their own experience of successful or unsuccessful attempts at flattery.

A more extended task would be to ask them to *script* their sketches after improvising, and then *rehearse* – in order to present a more polished performance.

Anansi and Tiger

A Jamaican tale

Princess Adowa was the most beautiful woman in the village. Both Anansi – part man, part spider – and Tiger wanted to be her husband.

'I will marry the one who proves himself to be the strongest.'

Tiger laughed. Everyone agreed that Tiger was stronger than a spider.

After that, no one saw Anansi for many days.

One day, Tiger was padding through the forest when he found Anansi resting under a tree.

'What are you doing here, Brother Anansi?'
'I have hurt my leg. See my walking stick? I am hiding here in shame. You, Brother Tiger, are so much stronger than me.'

Tiger laughed.

'If I am stronger than you, come with me to tell Princess Adowa so I may marry her.'
'Very well, Brother Tiger. I will come with you. But I have hurt my leg. Oh Beautiful Tiger, Magnificent Tiger, just one thing I ask.'
'What is that, Brother Anansi?'

'Carry me to the village on your powerful back.'
'It is true that my back is powerful. Very well, Brother Anansi. Climb on my back.'

Anansi climbed onto Tiger's back, and Tiger padded through the forest towards the village.

'Oh Beautiful Tiger, Magnificent Tiger, just one thing I ask.'
'What is that, Brother Anansi?'

'I left my stick under the tree and, without it, I cannot walk. You have such keen eyesight; won't you turn back and help me to find my stick?'
'It is true that my eyesight is keen. Very well, Brother Anansi.'

Tiger soon found the stick and gave it to Anansi, and, once more, Tiger padded through the forest towards the village.

'Oh Beautiful Tiger, Magnificent Tiger, just one thing I ask.'
'What is that, Brother Anansi?'

'I keep slipping on your fine sleek fur. Won't you cut a vine from the tree with your sharp claw so I can put it around your neck and hold on?'
'It is true that my fur is fine and sleek and that my claws are sharp. Very well, Brother Anansi.'

Tiger cut a vine with his sharp claw, and Anansi put it around Tiger's neck and held on. Tiger padded through the forest towards the village.

'Oh Beautiful Tiger, Magnificent Tiger, just one thing I ask.'
'What is that, Brother Anansi?'

'The vine keeps slipping on your fine sleek fur. Won't you hold the vine between your powerful teeth so I can hold on?'
'It is true that my teeth are powerful. Very well, Brother Anansi.'

Tiger took the vine between his teeth and Anansi held on. Tiger padded through the forest towards the village.

Soon they came to the edge of the village. Anansi took his stick and struck Tiger hard on his backside.

Tiger roared and ran forward into the village, Anansi holding on tight to the vine.

The people ran out of their houses to see Anansi riding on Tiger's back.

Once more, Anansi struck Tiger hard on his backside and Tiger roared in pain.

Princess Adowa came out of her house and saw that Anansi was stronger than Tiger.

Tiger knew that Anansi had won. Tiger bent his head down low.

Anansi climbed down from Tiger's back and tied him by the vine to the nearest tree. Anansi took Princess Adowa's hand and stepped inside her house.

Soon they were married.

Repetition of phrases with alterations

A telling technique

It is both challenging and fun for students to remember and repeat phrases which change each time.

Lazy Jack is one of the best-loved folk tales in the English tradition, and for good reason. I first heard it from my big sister Jan Coles, an expert storyteller and puppeteer.

To rehearse, choose mimed actions to go with '*She kicked Jack out of the house*' and '*Jack remembered his mother's words*' – to help the students join in with these repeated phrases early on in the story. They have to remember five different commands from the mother, so a mimed action for each one will help them.

Before telling

This is a tale with a lot of joining in, so play 'Mime a job' first – to get the students miming:

- First you mime a job yourself for the students to guess – firefighter, window cleaner, musician, soldier, fisherman, taxi driver, opera singer …
- Then they stand in pairs, alternating turning their back to the board – you write up the jobs one by one for the students facing the board to mime. The first pair to guess the job wins the round.

While telling

Use your rehearsed phrases and mimed actions. The students will soon pick up on the repeated pattern of Jack remembering his mother's last command beginning '*Next time …*'.

- Each time, the students need to remember along with Jack.
- If you slow down, pause and gesture before each refrain, you make it easy for them to participate verbally and physically in this choral storytelling.

Pause telling the story at the point when Jack starts carrying the donkey, and say: *We are nearly at the end of the tale. Already you're imagining how the story could finish. Discuss your ideas for the ending with your neighbour. Perhaps they will be different, or perhaps you can find one ending together.*

Now invite a willing volunteer to come to the front and tell their ending to the class, then ask: *Who would like to tell us a very different ending?*

- After about three endings have been told, the students can tell their endings again to a different partner.
- Here, they might borrow ideas from other students' endings, to enhance their own.

Finally, you tell the traditional ending to this popular tale.

After telling

Point out that Jack is portrayed as a fool in all Jack stories, but he always tries his best and never gives up, so he is rewarded in the end.

Ask the whole class: *Who do you feel for in this story, Jack or his mother? Why?*

Say: *Stand facing a partner. One of you is Jack – returning home just after you dropped the penny in the river. The other is Jack's mother – you want to know what happened. Are you going to be surprised that Jack lost the penny? How do you stand? What's your voice like? Make a still picture. 3–2–1 Action!*

Invite one or two volunteer pairs to act out their scene. The other students can comment on the performance and on the mother–son relationship.

To follow on, invite small groups of students to create a 'sequel' about what happened after the wedding – with Jack and his new wife, and possibly the father and Jack's mother.

- If these stories are written down, they can be read aloud.
- If they are devised orally, they can be told as stories or performed as dramas.

Finally, some students may wish to talk about what the story and sequel remind them of in their own families.

Lazy Jack
An English tale

Once upon a time, there was a boy called Jack.

His mother thought he was lazy and good for nothing, so one morning she kicked Jack out of the house and told him to find a job.

Jack got work with a builder, and at the end of the day Jack had built a fine wall. The builder gave Jack a penny.

As Jack was coming home, he tossed the penny and caught it, tossed the penny and caught it.

As he was crossing a bridge, he tossed the penny, and the penny fell in the river.

When he got home, he told his mother.
'You foolish boy,' said his mother. 'Next time, put it in your pocket.'

The next morning, she kicked Jack out of the house, and Jack got work with a dairy farmer.

Lazy Jack

At the end of the day, Jack had milked so many cows that the farmer gave him a jug of milk.

Jack remembered his mother's words – *'next time, put it in your pocket'* – so he poured the milk into his pocket, and walked home with milk running down his leg.

When he got home, he told his mother.
'You foolish boy,' said his mother. 'Next time, carry it on your head.'

The next morning, she kicked Jack out of the house, and Jack got work with a cheese-maker.

At the end of the day, Jack had made a lot of delicious strong cheese. The cheese-maker gave him a beautiful, big, round cheese.

Jack remembered his mother's words – *'next time, carry it on your head'* – so he carried the cheese on his head. It was a hot and sunny day and the cheese melted into his hair.

When he got home, he told his mother.
'You foolish boy,' said his mother. 'Next time, carry it in your hands.'

The next morning, she kicked Jack out of the house, and Jack got work with a cook, working in the kitchens of the big house. Jack washed up the pots and pans and looked after the cats that caught the rats.

At the end of the day, Jack had worked so hard that the cook gave him the big tom cat.

Jack remembered his mother's words – *'next time, carry it in your hands'* – so he carried the tom-cat in his hands, but the tom-cat was wild and bit and scratched until Jack let go and the cat ran off.

When he got home, he told his mother.
'You foolish boy,' said his mother. 'Next time, tie it with a piece of string and pull it home behind you.'

The next morning, she kicked Jack out of the house, and Jack got work with a butcher, chopping meat.

At the end of the day, Jack had worked so hard that the butcher gave him a whole side of lamb.

Jack remembered his mother's words – *'next time, tie it with a piece of string and pull it home behind you'* – so he tied it with a piece of string and pulled it home behind him. The meat was soon filthy, all covered in dust and mud.

When he got home, he told his mother.
'You foolish boy,' said his mother. 'Next time, carry it across your shoulders.'

The next morning, she kicked Jack out of the house, and Jack got work with a merchant, doing business from village to village. The merchant rode upon his horse and Jack followed on a donkey.

At the end of the day, Jack had done so well that the merchant gave him the donkey.

Jack remembered his mother's words – *'next time, carry it across your shoulders'*.

Jack had been working hard for a whole week and had grown into a fine strong young man. He bent down low under the donkey, and lifted it up. Jack carried the donkey across his shoulders.

I wonder if you can guess how this story finishes?

Now it happened that, in that village, there lived a rich man with his only daughter. She was a beautiful girl but, in her whole life, she had never laughed.

Her father had promised that whoever could make her laugh could marry her.

This girl happened to be looking out of the window when Jack came past, carrying the donkey across his shoulders.

As she watched, she felt something she had never felt before: a strange shaking inside, and her lips began to tremble.

She laughed, and she laughed, and she laughed, so loudly that her father came running to see what was happening.

He looked out of the window and called to Jack to stop.

Together, they went to Jack's mother, the girl riding on the donkey while Jack and her father walked alongside.

Jack's mother was amazed.

Soon Jack was married to the rich man's daughter, and he became a rich man.

They lived in a big house, and Jack's mother lived with them in great happiness until she died.

Repetition of rhymes

A telling technique

Rhymes are an enjoyable way for students to remember sounds and rhythms, and they are frequent in folk tales.

Juan and the Magic Tree is a Filipino folk tale with a plot common to many tales where the deserving hero is cheated of three magical objects then wins them back. The Filipino features – bolo knife, palm wine, fishing net – transport me straight to the tropical islands of South East Asia.

To rehearse, say the two repeated rhymes rhythmically, and imagine getting your students to join in. You could use a shaker to emphasise the rhythm.

Before telling

Ask the students to discuss in pairs their answers to the question *What do you expect from a friend?* then share their ideas as a class.

While telling

The first time you say the two rhymes, emphasise them by pausing momentarily, leaning forward, then saying them louder.

The second time, gesture with open hands to invite the students to say the rhymes along with you.

The last time, you can be quiet and let the students say them in your place.

After telling

Say to the whole class: *Stand in pairs. One of you is Juan and the other is Juan's friend.*
Juan: you have been living well for the last few weeks and sharing your fish and gold with the villagers.
Juan's friend: you haven't been to the village since you tricked Juan and were beaten by the stick. You are poor and you are hungry. You have come into the village to ask Juan to share some of what he has with you. You talk together for a couple of minutes.
Ready? 3–2–1 Action!

Ask volunteer pairs to show their conversations to the class for the listening students to comment.

To follow on, there is an opportunity here for a discussion of friendship and forgiveness.
- In groups, the students tell a story about a time they made up with a friend who they had previously fallen out with.
- The story can be true, partly true or completely made up. The other group members question them, before guessing how much is true.

Juan and the Magic Tree

A Filipino tale

'You're no good, Juan, where's the wood?
Where's the wood, Juan, you're no good.'

This is what Juan's mother said every day.

She gave him a sharp bolo knife and sent him from the village to fetch firewood.

Juan walked through the forest until he came to a tall and spindly tree. He lifted the bolo high in the air and was just about to start chopping, when the tree sang:

'Don't cut me, I'm a magic tree,
I'm a magic tree, Juan, don't cut me.'

'Why shouldn't I cut you?' asked Juan.
'I will give you a goat.'

The trunk of the tree split open, and out stepped a goat.
'Whenever you tickle the goat's beard, you will have gold.'

Juan led the magic goat between the trees. At the edge of the forest, Juan met his friend.
'What have you got there, Juan?'

Juan tickled he goat's beard and a pile of gold coins fell upon the ground.

'Let us celebrate,' said Juan's friend, 'I will buy some palm wine.'

His friend gave Juan first one glass of sweet palm wine, then another glass, and then a third glass.

Juan fell into a drunken stupor.

Quickly, his friend led the magic goat away and returned with another goat with a similar coat.

When Juan woke up, he led the goat back to his mother.

'You're no good, Juan, where's the wood?
Where's the wood, Juan, you're no good.'

'But look, mother, I have brought a magic goat that drops gold from its beard, see?'

Juan bent down and tickled the goat's beard, but there was no gold.

She was angry. She gave him the bolo again and sent him back off to fetch firewood.

Juan walked through the forest until he came to the same tree, tall and spindly. He lifted the bolo high in the air and was just about to start chopping, when the tree sang:

Juan and the Magic Tree

'Don't cut me, I'm a magic tree,
I'm a magic tree, Juan, don't cut me.'

'Why shouldn't I cut you?' asked Juan, 'The goat gave me gold just once.'
'I will give you a net.'

The highest branches of the tree shook, and down dropped a fishing net.

'Wherever you cast the fishing net, in treetop or on dry ground, it will come back full of fish.'

Juan carried the magic net between the trees. At the edge of the forest, Juan met his friend.
'What have you got there, Juan?'

Juan cast the fishing net between the trees and when he pulled it in, it was full of beautiful fish.

'Let us celebrate,' said Juan's friend, 'We will cook the fish and I will buy some more palm wine.'

The fish was delicious and his friend gave Juan first one glass of sweet palm wine, then another, and then a third.

Juan again fell into a drunken stupor.

Quickly, his friend took the magic net away and returned with another similar-looking net.

When Juan woke up, he carried the net back to his mother's house.

'You're no good, Juan, where's the wood?
Where's the wood, Juan, you're no good.'

'But look, mother, I have brought a magic fishing net. Wherever I cast it, it comes back full of fish, see?'

Juan cast the fishing net right there in the middle of the village, but when he pulled it in, the net was empty.

His mother was furious. She gave him the bolo again.
'Come back with wood or don't ever come back at all.'

Juan walked through the forest until he came to the same tree, tall and spindly. He lifted the bolo high in the air and was just about to start chopping, when the tree sang:

'Don't cut me, I'm a magic tree,
I'm a magic tree, Juan, don't cut me.'

'I will cut you down,' said Juan. 'The net gave me fish just once.'
'I have nothing more to give you,' said the tree, 'except a stick.'

Juan heard a branch snap above him, and a stick fell on the ground at his feet.

'What does it do?'
'I cannot tell you. Whoever is holding the stick will get what they deserve, when you call *Boombye Boomba!*'

Juan carried the stick between the trees. At the edge of the forest, Juan met his friend.

'What have you got there, Juan?' asked his friend, grabbing the stick from Juan.

'What does this stick do?'
'I don't know,' said Juan, 'but let's find out what you deserve. *Boombye Boomba!*'

The stick jumped out of his friend's hand, went three times round his head and started beating him on his back and on his bottom until he was black and blue.

'Make it stop! Make it stop!' cried Juan's friend.

'I'll make it stop,' said Juan, who was not so foolish after all, 'if you'll give me back my magic goat and magic net.'

The friend promised, and Juan ordered the stick to stop. Juan's friend fetched the goat and the net, and Juan took them and the stick back to his mother's house.

'You're no good, Juan, where's the wood?
Where's the wood, Juan, you're no good.'

Juan's mother took the magic stick from him. 'Is this all you could carry?'

Juan wondered what his mother deserved, and called *Boombye Boomba!*

The stick jumped out of his mother's hand, went three times round her head and was just about to start beating her when Juan ordered it to stop.

Juan tickled the magic goat's beard and gold coins fell upon the ground. He cast the magic net and it came back full of fish.

In the village, there was a great feast in celebration. Juan's mother was amazed, and never again spoke a word against him.

Juan lived the rest of his life in plenty because of the goat and the net.

And the magic stick came in useful, too.

Repetition of episodes

A telling technique

The students can be encouraged to tell the story along with you, where whole episodes are repeated word for word.

The Witch of Tavistock is a tale from Dartmoor, near where I live. Dartmoor is rich in folklore, and there are many tales of spirits, witches and strange apparitions. Because I know Dartmoor well, the images I have in my mind are closely tied to the landscapes I have walked through. This tale is retold from the version collected by V. Day Sharman in *Devon Folk Tales* (Nelson 1952) – out of print, but available from Read Books at Amazon UK.

To rehearse, focus on the rhythm of the 'three times repeated' episode, and use distinct voices for the three characters.
- Mime simple actions – such as knocking at the door – to reinforce the repetition of the verbal language.
- Use the same words, voices, rhythm and actions each time – adding to the magic and mystery of the story.

This will make it *possible* for the students to join in telling the episode the *second* time – and *easy* to say it along with you the *third* time.

Before telling

Set the scene of the story, using the information about Dartmoor above. You could also introduce Dartmoor National Park through student research on the internet: *www.dartmoor-npa.gov.uk*.

While telling

Invite the students to tell the repeated episodes the second and third time – by gesturing with an open hand.

Maintain the tempo of your storytelling, so that the students have to keep up with *you* – rather than *you* slowing down for *them*.

After telling

Discuss the fact that the story takes place over three full moons, and that the same episode is repeated three times.

Ask the students for the sequence of repeated events in one episode and, as they call them out, quickly draw on the board simple symbols to represent the following features of the story and link them together with arrows – to show the cyclical sequence of the episode:
- *hunger/full moon*
- *door*
- *running hare*
- *silver sixpence*
- *horse and hounds*
- *disappeared hare*
- *bread and meat*

For example:
- You can draw one simple circle to represent both the full moon and hunger (an empty plate) – this symbol both starts and ends the sequence.
- You can draw the disappeared hare as an empty space surrounded by flashes.

Say: *Turn to your partner and use the prompts on the board to take it in turns to tell the episode as you remember it – from 'the night of the full moon' to 'they were poor and hungry'.*

Ask pairs of students to discuss what advice they would give to the Boy, the Grandmother and the Lord of the Manor at the end of the story, and then discuss this as a class.

Find out which character different students feel most empathy with, and invite them to explain why – personally, I am often surprised that students feel sorry for the Lord of the Manor because he is a victim of deceit.

To follow on, point out that there may be regions that your students know well which are rich in mystery and folklore. Otherwise, they can find more Dartmoor tales on the internet.
- Ask them to research and prepare to tell a supernatural folk tale or legend they know for the next class.
- In the next lesson, put the students into small groups of those who have prepared different tales. If some have not come up with a tale, they can join the groups of those who have – and listen.

The Witch of Tavistock

A traditional tale from Devon, England

Dartmoor is a mysterious place with many tales of spirits, fairies and witches.

There was an old woman who lived with her young grandson in a simple cottage on the edge of Dartmoor, near the market town of Tavistock.

They had nothing. They were poor and hungry.

On the night of the full moon, the old woman told her grandson:
'Go to the Lord of the Manor. Knock at his door. Tell him there's a hare running across the moor. He will give you a silver sixpence.'

So the boy did as his grandmother had told him:

'Sir, there's a hare running across the moor.'
'A hare running across the moor, boy? Here's a silver sixpence.'

The Lord fetched his horse and hunting hounds, and soon he was riding across the moor. By the light of the moon, he could see a hare running fast and zigzagging left and right.

When his hounds were about to catch the hare on the edge of the moor near Tavistock, the hare just disappeared.

The old woman and her young grandson had bread and meat to eat because of the silver sixpence, but at the end of the month they had nothing.

Once more, they were poor and hungry.

On the night of the full moon, the old woman told her grandson:
'Go to the Lord of the Manor. Knock at his door. Tell him there's a hare running across the moor. He will give you a silver sixpence.'

So the boy did as his grandmother had told him:

'Sir, there's a hare running across the moor.'
'A hare running across the moor, boy? Here's a silver sixpence.'

The Lord fetched his horse and hunting hounds, and soon he was riding across the moor. By the light of the moon, he could see a hare running fast and zigzagging left and right. When his hounds were about to catch the hare on the edge of the moor near Tavistock, the hare just disappeared.

The old woman and her young grandson had bread and meat to eat because of the silver sixpence, but at the end of the month they had nothing.

Once more, they were poor and hungry.

On the night of the full moon, the old woman told her grandson:
'Go to the Lord of the Manor. Knock at his door. Tell him there's a hare running across the moor. He will give you a silver sixpence.'

So the boy did as his grandmother had told him:

'Sir, there's a hare running across the moor.'

But this time, the Lord of the Manor was ready and waiting.

As soon as the boy knocked, the door flew open and out he rode upon his horse, with the hounds running before him. They were upon the hare as soon as it appeared, but it managed to switch back and escape their sharp teeth.

Once more, the hounds caught up and were biting at the hare's legs and neck.

But now they were in the same place on the edge of the moor near Tavistock, where the old woman lived with her grandson, and the hare just disappeared.

The Lord of the Manor rode up to the simple cottage, leapt down from his horse, kicked open the door and ran inside.

There, in her bed, was the old woman, red-faced and panting. When he looked at her neck and arms, the Lord of the Manor saw the teeth marks of his hounds.

The old woman was taken to court and the judge found her guilty of being a witch and changing herself into the shape of a hare. But she said:
'I am poor. Without the money, my grandson would be dead from hunger.'

What do you think the judge should do?

The judge set her free, on condition that she never practised witchcraft again.

Perhaps she did, and perhaps she did not.

That would be another story.

Interacting with the characters

A telling technique

Stepping into the role of a character during your storytelling gives the students an opportunity to interact imaginatively with the story and with their teacher.

Bedd Gelert is a well-known legend from Snowdonia in North Wales, and Gelert's tomb (*Bedd Gelert* in Welsh) is there for you to visit. As with most legends, it is hard to trace its origins.

As the son of Welsh parents, I am proud to tell this stirring and tragic tale from the Land of my Fathers.

You can find another creative way into telling this story in *Once Upon a Time* by John Morgan and Mario Rinvolucri (Cambridge University Press 1983).

To rehearse, pay attention to the inner emotional world of the main character, which is described in this story – unlike in most folk tales.

- Make sure these emotions come across in your storytelling, but be subtle – until you step into the role of Llewellyn at the height of his anguish, and cry out:
  Oh monstrous hound, you have killed my only son! What shall I do?
- Llewellyn is a prince, so work on an appropriate posture and voice – and be prepared to stay in role as you listen and respond to your students' suggestions.

Before telling

Invite one or two students to give a personal example of the loyalty of a pet dog or a friend of theirs.

While telling

Just before Llewellyn finds the baby:

- Step into the role of the prince and cry out, as you rehearsed:
  Oh monstrous hound, you have killed my only son! What shall I do?
- Remain in role, turning to the students and appealing to them:
  What shall I do? This hound has killed my baby son! Tell me what I should do.

Imagine that the students are your conscience:

- Listen to different suggestions.
- Each time, ask – as Llewellyn – if the others agree.

It may be that some students predict that there will be a twist at the end of the tale.

When all the different suggestions have been made, step out of role – and continue to the end of the story. In this way, the students are like a chorus of advisors within the telling of the tale.

After telling

Ask pairs of students to discuss their interpretation of the *moral* of this story, before asking the whole class to reach a consensus regarding the *meaning* of the story.

Find an opportunity to teach the saying *'Don't jump to conclusions'* – and ask the students to think of a true story from their own life experience which illustrates it.

When a third of the students have remembered a story, ask them to form groups with two other students, whose task is to find out as much detail about the story as possible in three minutes.

- The groups of three then prepare to act out the story as a short roleplay.
- If there are only two characters involved, the person whose story it is can be the director and/or narrator.

After rehearsing it, each group performs their sketch.

As the others listen, their task is to work out the setting, the relationships involved and the nature of the misunderstanding.

After listening to each sketch, the whole class discuss their interpretations, before checking with the group who have just performed it. This leads to focused listening by peer students, which builds the speakers' confidence.

To follow on, say that there are similar tales in many cultures about loyal animals or servants, killed mistakenly by their masters. You can ask the students to find one and prepare to tell it in the next lesson.

Bedd Gelert

A Welsh legend

Prince Llewellyn loved to ride out in the Welsh mountains to hunt with his hounds.

His best and most loyal hound was Gelert, for he was not only the fastest, but he also led the pack and helped make Llewellyn the most respected huntsman in all of Wales.

Llewellyn had a year-old son, and one fine morning he kissed the little boy goodbye, left the castle and mounted his horse.

He blew his horn to summon his pack of hounds, and soon they were ready at the gates.

But Gelert was not there.

Llewellyn blew his horn again, but still Gelert did not come.

Llewellyn was angry. How would he hunt deer without his best hound?

A final time he blew his horn, and then he cracked the whip and rode out through the gates and into the mountains, the hounds baying out in front.

Gelert was not among them.

All day long, Llewellyn tracked a noble stag but, without his best hound Gelert, he returned at the end of the day empty-handed.

He approached the castle in the twilight and found Gelert at the gates, running forward to greet him.

Llewellyn, still angry, shouted at the hound and jumped down from his horse.

At that moment, he saw the red blood dripping from Gelert's mouth.

Llewellyn froze, and looked along the trail of blood to the open door of the castle.

Suddenly he remembered how much his young son loved to play with this favourite hound, and a terrible thought entered his head.

He ran to door and all the way to his young son's nursery, the hound following behind, yelping.

Inside the room, all was chaos: tables and chairs on their sides. To his horror, Llewellyn saw his young son's cradle overturned, the sheets stained with blood.

But nowhere could he find the little child.

'Oh monstrous hound, you have killed my only son! What shall I do?'

He drew his hunting knife and stabbed Gelert through the heart.

And as the hound lay dying, Llewellyn heard a sound, the cry of a young child.

He turned over the cradle, and there was his own son, safe and untouched, and next to him a great wolf, dead, with its throat ripped out, covered in blood.

Too late, Llewellyn learnt that Gelert had stayed behind to protect his only son.

The hound had fought and killed the wolf to save his master's child, and now Llewellyn had stabbed this most loyal hound.

He took Gelert gently in his arms, and the hound, looking at him with love and loyalty, died.

Prince Llewellyn buried Gelert outside the castle walls within sight of Snowdon, the highest mountain in all of Wales, and built a grave out of rocks.

The grave is still there to this day, where every passing traveller can see Bedd Gelert, the grave of Gelert.

Interacting with the students

A telling technique

You can interact directly with the students as an integral part of the telling of a story – by asking for advice, for solutions to problems, or for predictions.

How to Weigh an Elephant is a tale known to all Chinese students from a young age; it was told to me in class by a young Chinese woman. Cao Chong (196–208 CE) was the son of warlord Cao Cao of the Han Dynasty, and is well known as a child prodigy who died young.

To rehearse, it is a good idea to imagine the young prodigy Cao Chong going through the process of weighing the elephant step by step in your mind's eye.

Before telling

Tell the students that you are going to tell them a story that happened in China nearly 2,000 years ago.

While telling

When you ask for the students' suggestions for ways of weighing the elephant, see it as part of the storytelling. You are not 'interrupting' the story to interact with the students – rather, this interaction is very much a *part* of this story.

Make sure all the students listen closely to all the suggestions, by encouraging them to look at the person talking.
- Avoid rephrasing the suggestions *yourself* – unless you feel that most of the students have not understood.
- Avoid accepting or refusing suggestions – just ensure that everyone has had a chance to offer a solution. *They* can evaluate *each other's* suggestions.

Now continue with the story, whether the students have solved the problem in the same way as in the story – or not.

After telling

Get the students to explain back to you the process of weighing the elephant, step by step.
- Challenge them to explain the process to someone from another class or from outside.
- To get ready to do this, they can rehearse going through the process in pairs – while they imagine seeing Cao Chong in their mind's eye, just as you did.

In the next class, find out how successfully they managed to give instructions on 'how to weigh an elephant'!

To follow on, the students can research Archimedes' Principle, to understand the physical laws behind Cao Chong's method.

How to Weigh an Elephant
A tale from Ancient China

Nearly two thousand years ago, Cao Cao, the Emperor of China, was presented with an elephant.

'I must know the weight of this extraordinary creature,' he declared.

But none of his wise advisors could work out how to weigh such an enormous beast, and the Emperor became angry.

The Emperor's six-year-old son, Cao Chong, looked at the elephant and spoke up:

'It is easy, father. Come down to the water's edge and let me show you.'

Can you imagine how Cao Chong weighed the elephant?

'I need an empty boat, a piece of chalk, a pile of rocks and some weighing scales … and bring me a banana.'

Still the Emperor and the wisest advisors in the whole of China could not see how Cao Chong would weigh the elephant.

Can you?

Cao Chong stepped onto the boat, peeled the banana and held it up so that the elephant followed him.

The boat went down low into the water. The boy stepped back onto the land, reached over and drew a chalk line on the side of the boat just above the water.

Then he led the elephant back onto the shore and fed it the banana.

He told servants to load the empty boat with rock after rock, until the boat went down to exactly the same level as before.

Each rock was then unloaded and weighed separately.

The weights were added together and, finally, clever Cao Chong told his father the Emperor the exact weight of the elephant.

Emperor Cao Cao was delighted.

And his young son's fame spread far and wide.

Interacting through interruptions

A telling technique

If students question you about a story as you tell it, the storytelling can be more spontaneous, energetic and entertaining. The students will have a real sense of creating the story with you.

Cloud Eating is a tale told by the Bushmen of the Kalahari in Southern Africa. This is my retelling of the version in *South-African Folk Tales* by James A. Honey (1910) – out of print, but available free at *www.sacred-texts.com/afr/saft/*.

To rehearse this simple story, remember that you need to know it well enough to be able to tell it while being heavily quizzed. Generally, the students enjoy the opportunity to 'outdo' their teacher and will try to prevent you from finishing the tale.

Before telling

Tell the students you are going to tell a short myth tale from the Bushmen of Southern Africa.

- Ask if they can name any scavenging animals which have paws and live in Southern Africa.
- Make sure jackals and hyenas are mentioned.

Nominate a timekeeper, and say: *I'm going to tell you a very short tale about Brother Jackal and Sister Hyena, but you're going to try and stop me – by asking me as many questions as you can about what I tell you during the story.*

- *If I finish the story in two minutes, I win and you lose.*
- *If I haven't finished the story in two minutes, I lose and you win.*

Ready? 3–2–1 Go!

While telling

Tell the story as best you can while answering all the questions the students ask – as long as they are relevant to the story (ignore the others).

- You'll have to make up most of your answers on the spot using your imagination.
- If a student asks *Why doesn't Hyena jump on the cloud with Jackal?* you could say that she wanted to be safe, or that she wasn't quick enough – or whatever springs to mind.

Tell the tale a second time, from start to finish – this time without being interrupted.

Incorporate some of the details that came out of answering the students' questions, For example:
Brother Jackal jumped onto the cloud and began to eat, but Hyena was too slow and was left behind on the ground.

After telling

Now ask the students to retell their version of the story to each other in pairs, encouraging them to find voices for Jackal and Hyena. The fact that they have directly influenced the way this tale is told gives them a sense of ownership.

To follow on, tell the students that this is a 'pourquoi' story (a kind of creation myth) which explains why hyenas' hind legs are shorter than their front legs.

Ask them to make up their own *pourquoi* stories, explaining a physical feature of an animal – why elephants have long trunks, for example – to tell them to the class in the next lesson.

Cloud Eating

A tale from Southern Africa

Brother Jackal and Sister Hyena watched a cloud rising.

Brother Jackal jumped onto the cloud and began to eat. 'Mmm, it tastes like fat.'

'Brother Jackal, you're rising too high,' laughed Sister Hyena. 'Hahaha! Jump down and I'll catch you.'

Brother Jackal jumped down, and Sister Hyena caught him safely in her paws.

'Look, Sister Hyena. Another cloud is rising. Jump onto it and taste it!'

Sister Hyena jumped onto the cloud and began to eat. 'Mmm, it tastes like fat. Hahaha!'

Sister Hyena rose higher and higher, eating the delicious cloud.

'Brother Jackal, I've risen too high. Hahaha! Will you catch me when I jump down?'

'I'll catch you, Sister Hyena.'

Brother Jackal held out his paws and watched Sister Hyena coming down fast.

At the last moment, Brother Jackal jumped out of the way, crying, 'Oh, I've got a thorn in my paw!'

Sister Hyena landed heavily on her back paws.

Ever since that time, all hyenas have short back legs.

Interacting through riddles

A telling technique

Logical and lateral thinkers are eager to work out solutions to riddles, which are a common feature in folk tales from many cultures.

A Question of Brains is a tale from Lincolnshire in Eastern England, and I cannot deny that every time I tell it, I see my own marriage.

To rehearse this tale, be sure to put special emphasis on the riddles – so that the students can begin to work out the solutions before the end.

Before telling

Set the students the riddle below, and ask them to discuss the solution in pairs.

We never break, we never wear out.
You give us away and still you have us.
Each time you give us away, we get better.
And if you don't give us away, we are of no use.
What are we?

You might need to give some of the students extra clues. When everyone knows that the solution is 'Stories', explain that the story you are going to tell is a *riddle tale*.

While telling

When the students are listening to the story, they will be silently trying to guess the solutions to the riddles. Wait until the end of the story, and pause just before the young woman answers each of the riddles – to allow them to call out *their* solutions. For example:
'What runs but has no legs is … a river.'

After telling

Discuss the fact that riddles feature in traditional stories in many cultures.
- Ask the students in pairs to remember and practise posing the three riddles in the story.
- Ask the same pairs to remember any other riddles they know and, together, to choose a short one for the other students to answer. Both partners should rehearse posing the riddle.

Split the pairs and invite everyone to stand up and move from partner to partner, posing their riddles but not giving away the solutions – unless they are guessed correctly.

After a few minutes, find out which students' riddles are hardest to solve. Ask a few of those students to pose their riddles for the whole class to solve. Finally, discuss as a whole class what makes a good riddle.

To follow on, pose the students another riddle. For example: *What gets wetter and wetter the more it dries?* (A towel.)

Ask them to come to the next class with a new riddle for the others. There are many riddle sites they can look at on the internet. For example:
riddlesbrainteasers.com/category/riddles

A Question of Brains
An English folk tale

Some men are foolish some of the time. Some men are never foolish. Some men are foolish all of the time.

Once, there was a young man who had no brains.
He went to his mother: 'Mother, what am I going to do, I've got no brains.'
And she said: 'Boy, I'm an old woman and soon I'm going to die. You must get some brains.'
'How can I get some brains?'
'Go up the hill to find the wise old woman.'

He climbed up the hill until he came to the cave where the old woman lived.
'I need some brains.'
'Well I can't give you any brains,' she said. 'You'll have to find the brains yourself.'
'I don't how to get brains. Tell me!'

The old woman said: 'Bring me the heart of the one you love most in the world.'

The young man went back down the hill and he said to his mother: 'The wise old woman says I have to bring her the heart of the one I love most, but I don't know what that is!'
And his mother said: 'Tell me, boy, what do you really want right now?'
'Do you know what I'd love? I'd love a bacon sandwich.'
'Well, bacon comes from a pig! Kill the pig, and you can take the heart of the pig.'

So he killed the pig, and he cooked the bacon, and he ate a bacon sandwich, and then he took the heart in a bag and started walking up the hill.

A Question of Brains

Up the hill he went until he came to the cave of the old woman. 'Here! I've got the heart of my pig. That's the one I love most in the world.'

'Let us see,' said the old woman, 'if now you have some brains. I will ask you a question, and the question is this:

What runs but has no legs?'

'I don't know! How can I get some brains? Tell me!'
The old woman said: 'Bring me the heart of the one you love most in the world.'

So the young man went down the hill and back to his mother. 'Mother, I couldn't answer her question; I've got no brains.'
'Oh son,' said his mother. 'You must get some brains soon, for now I am going to die.'

And his mother closed her eyes, and she died.

The young man started to cry: 'Oh my mother!'

He wept, he cried, he moaned for day after day after day. 'I love my mother so much. I love my mother most in the world!'

And he picked up his mother's body.
'I can't take out her heart, but her heart is inside her body.'

So he put his mother into a sack, and he put the sack onto his shoulder, and he started to climb up the hill to the old woman, but he was very sad.

Finally, he came to the cave of the old woman.

'My mother is in this sack and I love her more than anything else in the world.'

'Well,' said the old woman. 'Let us see if now you have some brains. I'm going to ask you another question, and the question is this:

What shines like gold but is not gold?'

'Well I don't know, I've got no brains!'

And the young man walked back down the hill, and there he stayed at home and he didn't know what to do. He didn't know how to clean, he didn't know how to cook, he didn't know how to do anything.

One day, along came a neighbour, a lovely young woman.

'Why are you so sad?'
'Oh I can't do anything, I've got no brains!'
'Well, your house is dirty and you've got no food, let me help you.'

And the young woman started to cook, and she started to clean, and she started to help around the house. And, little by little, they got to know each other and, slowly, they started to fall in love.

And he told her about the old woman up on the hill, and how she asked him questions that he couldn't answer.

And when she heard these questions, she said:
'My heart is yours. Let's go together!'

So, arm in arm, they walked up the hill to the cave of the old woman.

'I love her more than anything else in the world,' said the young man.
'Well,' said the old woman, 'Let us see if now you have some brains. *What runs but has no legs?*'

'I know the answer,' said the young woman: 'What runs but has no legs is a river.'

'That's right,' said the old woman, *'And what shines like gold but is not gold?'*
'I know the answer,' said the young woman: 'What shines like gold but is not gold is the Sun.'

'True,' said the old woman, 'and here's one more question. *What starts off with no legs, then has four legs and ends up with two legs?*'

'That's impossible!' cried the young man.

'Let me think,' said the young woman. 'What starts off with no legs, then has four legs and ends up with two legs is a frog!'
'Correct,' said the old woman of the hill.

'Now give me my brains!' said the young man.
'I don't need to give you any brains. Your brains are standing right next to you. She's got brains enough for you both.'

'Well,' said the young woman, 'better a foolish husband than no husband at all. Come on and let's get married.'

And that's how the foolish young man got his brains.

Interacting through different cultures

A telling technique

The students are told two short folk tales from different cultures – and look for similarities.

The Three Golden Hairs is a Romanian tale I read in the wonderful book *Women Who Run With The Wolves* by the storyteller and psychoanalyst Clarissa Pinkola Estés (Ballantine Books 1992).

Jackal and the Shining Child is a tale from Southern Africa, which I found with the title 'Why has Jackal a long, black stripe on his back?' published in *South-African Folk Tales* by James A. Honey in 1910 – out of print, but available free at *www.sacred-texts.com/afr/saft/*.

To rehearse these two short myth tales, say them slowly and simply, focusing on the similarities between the two.

Before telling

Tell the students that you are going to tell them two short folk tales, one told in Romania and one told in Southern Africa – and that they should listen for similarities.

While telling

Pause only briefly between the two tales, so that the students can easily notice the similarities.

After telling

Ask the students, in pairs, to talk about the similarities they noticed between the two stories.

After a minute, they all pool their ideas.

They might mention the following:
- Myth type stories.
- The Sun in human form.
- The Sun character needs help.
- The Shining Child.
- Heat as an important feature.
- Hair/fur is burned/scorched.
- That the character is the Sun is only revealed at the end.
- Sunrise at the ending.
- Renewal.
- The offering/sacrifice means that the Sun will rise.

To follow on, the students can find another short folk tale featuring the Sun and prepare to tell it for the next class. They can search on the internet, or choose from the stories below – which all come from different traditions.

- Why the Sun and the Moon live in the Sky (Africa) *www.worldoftales.com/African_folktales/African_Folktale_10.html*
- Sun, Moon and Wind go out to Dinner (India) *www.worldoftales.com/Asian_folktales/Indian_folktale_27.html*
- The Wind and the Sun (Aesop) *www.taleswithmorals.com/aesop-fable-the-wind-and-the-sun.htm*
- The Sun and her Daughter (Native American-Cherokee) *www.firstpeople.us/FP-Html-Legends/TheDaughterOfTheSun-Cherokee.html*

The Three Golden Hairs

A Romanian tale

As the light fades at the end of the day, a white-haired old man steps towards the forest, holding a lantern up in front of him to light the way.

He moves slowly, bent over because of his great age.

His eyes are rheumy and he can hardly see, as he stumbles over tree roots and knocks against overhanging branches.

Ahead of him in the darkening forest, a small light glows from a cottage.

The door opens, the lantern flame goes out and he falls into the arms of a woman.

She closes the door and carries the ancient man to the fireplace, and sits rocking him gently in her arms.

'There there,' she says. 'There there.'

As she holds him and rocks him, the old man's years fall away. By the darkest hour of the night, he has become a strong young man.

'There there,' she says. 'There there.'

Before the first light of dawn, he has become a young boy with shining eyes and golden hair.

'There there,' she says. 'There there.'

She plucks three golden hairs from the child's head and casts them into the fireplace.

He climbs down from her lap and runs lightly to the door.

As he opens the door, the shining child looks lovingly back at his mother, and then leaps into the air and rises as the morning sun.

Jackal and the Shining Child

A myth from Southern Africa

Jackal finds a shining child sitting at the side of the path.

'Have your people left you behind?' asks Jackal.

Jackal takes the brightly shining child on his back and runs along the path, searching for the child's people all night long.

The child is so hot that Jackal's coat is scorched, but Jackal keeps running.

'You're burning me!' cries Jackal, and he tries to shake the shining child off his back.

But the child is stuck fast.

Finally, the shining child lets go and rises into the sky as the morning sun.

Jackal is left with a long black stripe on his back.

Interacting through personalisation

A telling technique

The students will be engaged by the truths revealed in traditional stories when they link these stories to their personal experience.

The Lost Axe is a concise Taoist tale from China by Lieh Tzu. I read it first in Jane Yolen's *Favorite Folktales from Around the World* (Pantheon 1986).

To rehearse, tell this tale as if it happened to *you*:
- You are going to try to make your students believe that you are the suspicious neighbour in this traditional Chinese tale – so you need to prepare carefully in order to tell it from your own perspective.
- You can add a few details – such as a specific recent date, location and the name of the boy, as well as a little description – so that your students will believe you.

If you don't think your students can imagine you using an axe, choose a different tool!

Before telling

Instead of getting the students 'ready to listen' – as you would for most of the stories you tell – introduce this story as you might introduce an interesting anecdote that happened to you 'just the other day':
'I want to tell you about something strange that happened to me last weekend …'

While telling

Pause when your suspicion is at its height, and ask the students what they would do in your shoes.
- Get a number of different suggestions from different students.
- Then tell the end of the tale.

After telling

Ask the students to talk in pairs about the meaning of the story, and how they feel about it (at this stage, they should still believe it's a true story that happened to you).

Now ask the whole class:
Who thinks this really happened to me? Why/Why not?

Get a few students to explain their guesses.

Finally, tell the original tale and admit that you adapted it – so it is not 'true', after all, but there is much 'truth' in it!

Open up a class discussion about how traditional tales are ways of teaching moral behaviour.

To follow on, find out which students have a true story to tell about a time they were suspicious of someone. Those students without stories can go from student to student, listening and remembering each of the stories. That way:
- Each storyteller tells their story three or four times.
- Each listener listens to three or four different students' stories.

The listeners then tell the whole class:
- *Which of the stories was the most surprising? Why?*
- *Which story was the funniest?*
- *Which was the most thought-provoking?*

The Lost Axe

A Chinese tale

A man was chopping wood with his axe near his home.

The next day, he couldn't find his axe.

He noticed his neighbour's son, and thought that perhaps he had stolen his axe.

The boy looked at him in a strange way, and walked in a strange way.

He was sure his neighbour's son had stolen the axe.

The next day, the man found his axe in the place where he himself had left it.

When he noticed his neighbour's son again, the boy looked at him like any other boy, and walked like any other boy.

Chapter Two
Creative ways into and out of a story

'The more I teach, the more I'm noticing the link between learning and mental imagery. Storytelling – the most powerful kickstart for imagination that I know of – is the fuel by which images are born and flourish.'

Nick Bilbrough
Teacher, teacher trainer and author

Technique	Story	Page
From story to lesson	*The Teacher*	70
Predicting the story	*Little Dog, Panther and Monkey*	71
Asking and imagining	*The Small Bird's Wisdom*	72
Imagining and improvising	*Aldar Kose Tricks the Bai*	74
Freeze!	*Dongguo and the Wolf*	76
Act it out!	*The Coat*	78
Responding in role	*Garuda and Turtle*	80
Responding with a task	*The Snowgirl*	82
Responding with a gift	*Mbongoro*	84
Responding personally	*The Fly*	86
Exploring metaphor	*The Snake Wife*	88
Exploring mental imagery	*After the Fire*	90
Exploring meaning	*The Ferryman and the Grammar Teacher*	92

From story to lesson

A telling technique

A short relevant folk tale can introduce a new topic and stimulate the students' imaginations.

The Teacher is a Nasrudin Hodja tale I have adapted to a classroom setting. This 'wise fool' features in thousands of tales across Asia, North Africa, the Balkans and Russia.

To rehearse, emphasise the repeated question *Do you know what you're going to learn today?* Imagine *yourself* as the teacher in the story and *your students* as the students.

Before telling

If this story is used to introduce a topic, you need to do nothing before telling it, other than making sure everyone is ready!

While telling

The repetition of the question *Do you know what you're going to learn today?* is key in this story. If you pause momentarily before saying it – and gesture to the students to say it along with you on the second and third occasions – this will help them remember the question.

After telling

Allow the students a few moments to digest the story, before they talk about its meanings with their neighbours and then with the whole class.

Give them a choice as to how they answer the following questions about the day's lesson – they can write down, draw or make a mental note of their responses:
Do you know what you're going to learn today?
How much does the teacher decide what happens in the class?
How much do the students decide what happens in the class?
Do you want the teacher to be in complete control of what happens in the class? Why/why not?
How much can students teach and learn from each other?

Give them a few minutes to discuss their responses in pairs, and then listen to the whole class.
- Their answers will be influenced by their educational culture – you might draw attention to this.
- You also have an opportunity to share *your* thoughts and *your* approach to teaching.

To follow on, the students can work in like-minded groups – or pairs or individually (you could let them choose) – to prepare a short presentation: a talk, a sketch, a poem, a song, a poster, or even a documentary video featuring brief clips of different students giving their opinions direct to camera.

The Teacher

An adaptation of a traditional Turkish story

Nasrudin was a wise fool.

Once, he got a new job as an English teacher.

On the first morning, he walked into the classroom, stood at the front and asked the students:
'Do you know what you're going to learn today?'

The students looked at him and answered:
'No.'

Nasrudin walked to the door, turned, and said:
'Well, if you don't know what you're going to learn today, why am I here?'

And he left.

The students didn't understand.

The next morning, Nasrudin walked into the classroom, stood at the front, and asked the students:
'Do you know what you're going to learn today?'

The students were ready. They answered:
'Yes.'

Nasrudin walked to the door, turned, and said:
'Well, if you know what you're going to learn today, why am I here?'

And he left.

The students were confused.

On the third morning, the classroom was completely full. Students from all the other classes wanted to know what the strange new teacher would do.

Nasrudin walked into the classroom, stood at the front, and asked the students:
'Do you know what you're going to learn today?'

The students were ready.

Half of them said:
'Yes.'
And the other half said:
'No.'

Nasrudin walked to the door, turned, and said:
'Well, if half of you know what you're going to learn today and half of you don't know, those who know can tell those who don't know. Why am I here?'

And he left.

Predicting the story

A telling technique

When the students have predicted what might happen in a story, they are likely to be engaged when you *tell* it. Inviting them to predict – before they listen – will help them focus on the story to find out how accurate their predictions are.

Little Dog, Panther & Monkey is a tale told to me in Spanish by María Nieves López from Venezuela.

To rehearse this tale, focus on distinct postures, mannerisms and voices for the characters:

- Little Dog (the nervous but quick-thinking hero)
- Panther (the slow-witted predator)
- Monkey (the foolish tale-teller)

Before telling

Say: *I'm going to tell you a Venezuelan story set deep in the forest, called 'Little Dog, Panther and Monkey'. Before you listen, what do you imagine Little Dog wants, what do you imagine Panther wants, and what do you imagine Monkey wants? Tell a partner.*

While telling

Stop at the moment when Panther is about to attack Little Dog for the second time, and say: *The story is nearly at its end. What's going to happen? Listen to your partner's ideas.*

After a minute, bring the class together to listen to different ideas from some different students and say: *I wonder if any of you guessed the traditional Venezuelan ending?*

Now the students are ready to listen to the original ending.

After telling

Ask pairs of students to talk about what lessons can be learned from this tale and then, as a class, find out what ideas they had – before telling them what they say in Venezuela:
Don't be frightened of strangers, like Panther was.
Don't be a gossip, like Monkey was.
Be like Little Dog – use your imagination!

To follow on, ask the students what traditional folk tales they know that are set in a forest.

Ask them to research forest folk tales on the internet and prepare to each tell one folk tale, myth or superstition to the other students. They can do this in small groups, if you or they prefer.

Little Dog, Panther & Monkey

A tale from Venezuela

Little Dog was lost, deep in the forest.

There, among the tall trees, Little Dog was afraid. He had always been looked after and fed, and now he was alone.

He searched and searched for a way out of the forest, but he became more and more lost.

Monkey was up in the tree, but he offered no help.

There on the ground, Little Dog found a pile of gleaming white bones, and he wondered what creature had died there, alone in the forest.

As he stood before the bones, he caught the scent of an animal on the prowl. Panther was coming towards Little Dog from behind.

Panther had never seen a little dog before. What a tasty meal this creature would make!

Just as Panther was about to pounce, Little Dog licked one of the bones and said, loud and clear:
'What a tasty meal! How delicious panther meat is!'

Panther turned and fled between the trees.

Monkey watched everything from up in the tree and thought Little Dog was too clever for his own good. No one in the forest was allowed to be cleverer than Monkey!

Monkey went swinging through the trees, and called down to Panther: 'You've been tricked. That little dog ate no panther. You should go back and eat him.'

When Panther heard this, he felt foolish and became angry.

With Monkey riding on his back, Panther came prowling back towards Little Dog, ready to catch and eat him.

But Little Dog had such a good nose that he could smell both Panther and Monkey coming.

What could he do?

Little Dog said, loud and clear:
'Why, it's such a long time since I sent Monkey off to bring me another panther to eat! And I'm so hungry!'

Panther turned and fled between the trees so fast, terrified of Little Dog and furious with Monkey, who held on tightly to the fur on his back.

That day, it was not Little Dog that Panther had for his supper.

Asking and imagining

A telling technique

If students have found out about and imagined a story beforehand, they will listen closely to you telling it and compare their own version.

The Small Bird's Wisdom is a short and powerful Polish wisdom tale translated by Professor D. L. Ashliman under the title *The Three Proverbs* – on his remarkably comprehensive folk tales web resource: *www.pitt.edu/~dash/type0150.html*

To rehearse this story, which is largely a dialogue between the rich man and the small bird, give the two characters distinct voices. When you speak as the rich man, try the following:

- Hold out your closed hand and look at it – as if the bird is there.
- Alternatively, look up, as if you are talking to the small bird sitting in the tree.

Make sure that you know the story well enough to be able to spontaneously answer questions the students ask.

Before telling

Say: *The Small Bird's Wisdom is a Polish story about a rich man who catches a small bird in his garden, but the only thing the small bird wants is its freedom. Ask me as many questions as you can about the story in one minute – and then you can tell the story as you imagine it.*
Ready? Ask!

You answer the questions briefly and truthfully, without giving away the whole story. If you can't answer a question, say you can't.

After the one minute of questions and answers, give pairs of students a few minutes to tell each other the story together, as they imagine it.

Once they have finished, ask the pairs to split, get new pairs to listen to each other telling their versions of *The Small Bird's Wisdom* – and compare them.

While telling

When you are telling the story, use your distinct 'character voices' to make it clear:

- When you are speaking as the rich man.
- When you are speaking as the small bird.

After telling

Ask pairs of students to compare *their* versions with the traditional Polish story you have just told.

To follow on, explain that *The Small Bird's Wisdom* is a tale about freedom. Ask the students to discuss in small groups what freedom means to them.

- In what ways are they free?
- In what ways is their freedom constrained?

They can then write sentences beginning 'Freedom is …' and display these sentences on the classroom wall.

They could also research The Universal Declaration of Human Rights and organisations such as Amnesty International.

The Small Bird's Wisdom

A Polish tale

A rich man was walking through his richly-scented springtime garden and, there, he found a small bird caught in a net.

He took it in his hand and, to his surprise, the small bird spoke.

'Set me free. There is nothing I love more than my freedom.'

'Why should I set you free?' asked the rich man.

'I am too small to eat. My feathers are grey. I am not pretty. I do not sing. Please set me free.'

'What will you give me in return for your freedom?'

'I will give you three pieces of advice.'

'I will listen to your advice. Then I will decide whether to give you your freedom.'

'First, do not wish for what you cannot have.
Second, do not try to change what has already happened.
Third, do not believe in what is impossible.'

'Wise words indeed!' said the rich man.

He opened his hand, and the small bird flew up to the branch of a tree overhead.

The rich man heard the small bird laughing.

'Small bird, why do you laugh? Are you laughing at me?'

'Why yes. What you do not know is that, inside me, I have a diamond the size of a chicken's egg.'

For a moment, the rich man could not speak. His eyes grew dark. His heart stopped beating. He could hardly catch his breath.

Finally he said:
'Small bird, come back to me. Now it is springtime and all is well, soon summer will come and go, but then winter will come and it will be cold. You will be hungry. The snow will be deep, and you will have nothing to eat. You will starve to death in the cold. Come back to me and I will look after you. I will keep you warm and feed you through the long winter.'

The rich man held out his open hand to the bird, but the bird just laughed.

'Are you still laughing at me?'

'Why yes. You are like all men. So soon you have forgotten my advice:
Do not wish for what you cannot have – you cannot have me, for there is nothing I love more than my freedom.
Do not try to change what has already happened – you have already set me free, and you cannot change this.
Do not believe in what is impossible – how would it be possible for a small bird like me to have a diamond the size of a chicken's egg inside?'

And, laughing, the small bird flew away.

Imagining and improvising

A telling technique

Before you tell students a story, they can do improvised drama roleplay based on information you give them about characters and events.

Aldar Kose Tricks the Bai is the best-known Kazak folk tale about the popular legendary hero, Aldar Kose. Kazak student Assiya Omarova delighted her international student friends by telling it at a storytelling evening I recently hosted at the University of Exeter.

To rehearse this tale, try miming the actions expressively – such as throwing open your coat, exchanging coats, taking the purse of gold and climbing onto a horse.

Before telling

Say: *Imagine you are freezing cold in the snow, wearing a thin old coat full of holes. You meet someone rich who is wearing a thick warm coat. You really need it. Unfortunately, you have no money and nothing of value. What could you say to this rich person to get the coat?*

Write all the ideas that the students come up with on the board, so they are clearly displayed. These may include examples of begging and pleading, offering to return favours in the future, blackmail, etc.

Say: *Now stand facing a partner. Use words, no physical contact.*
- *One of you is really cold, and you are going to try to get your partner's coat – using as many different ideas as you can.*
- *Your partner is going to refuse and make an excuse every time.*
3–2–1 Action!

While telling

Mime the actions as you tell the story – so that your students will easily be able to act out the story in mime themselves afterwards.

After telling

Ask pairs of students to compare the strategies used by Aldar Kose with the strategies *they* used in the improvised drama roleplay they did earlier.

Invite the students, in the same pairs as before, to act out the whole story – this time in mime.
- You might retell the story at the same time as they do this.
- They will not be speaking, so they can be encouraged to act with a lot of physical expression: the clever trickster Aldar Kose and the rich self-important Bai need to show or hide how cold they are, describe their horses, make and refuse offers, etc.

Next, the same pairs can act out the story, this time with actions *and* dialogue together.

A few pairs can show their version of the story to the whole class. Before they do this, ask the other students to notice differences from *their own* version, and to be ready to tell the pair afterwards what they enjoyed about their performance.

To follow on, ask the students to remember a time they tricked someone, or a time someone tricked them. Tell them to think about the following:
When and where did it happen?
Who was involved?
What was the trick?
What was the result?
How did it make them feel?

When a third of the class have a story to tell, put all the students in groups of three, with two students who don't have a tale in mind. These students need to listen and ask questions and check details, in order to be able to retell the story as well as they can – in the next stage.

When all the groups are ready, ask the students to leave their groups and form new groups of three. Each student should retell the trickster story which was told in their former group.

There are thousands of comic tales about tricksters like Aldar Kose in folk tales and jokes all over the world. The students might know some examples of trickster tales – or they can research and prepare to tell one in the next class.

Aldar Kose Tricks the Bai

A story from Kazakhstan

It was deepest winter on the Steppes of Kazakhstan, and clever Aldar Kose was on his poor old horse, trudging slowly through the snow.

His old coat was full of holes, seventy in total, and kept nothing of the cold out.

Riding toward him, Aldar Kose saw the Bai, the rich landowner, dressed in his thick fur coat and hat, seated proudly astride his fine horse.

Aldar Kose threw his coat open, and sang a song in praise of sunshine.

'Why, Aldar Kose, do you hold your coat open when it is so cold? Aren't you freezing?' asked the Bai.

'This coat keeps me too warm. It is a magic coat. The cold air comes in one hole and out another, so all the heat stays in.'

'A magic coat? How did you get this magic coat?'

'My father gave this enchanted coat to me, so that I should never be cold.'

The Bai looked closely at the coat.

'My coat is made of the finest fur, and yet I will offer it to you in exchange for your magic coat.'

'If I could exchange it, perhaps I would. But did I not tell you that it was my father who gave it to me himself? This magic coat would be hard to give away.'

'I'm not asking you to give it away,' said the Bai. 'You can have my hat as well as my coat. Here, feel the thickness of the fur.'

Aldar Kose had one eye on the Bai's coat, but the other was on his fine strong horse.

'My father told me on his deathbed that this coat should stay in my possession. He warned me about the coat … but now I forget what exactly he warned me …'

'You are trying my patience. I will have the coat. Take my coat, my hat, and my horse as well, in exchange for yours. This is my final offer.'

'But my father …'

'How dare you refuse me? I'm the richest man in the land! Take this purse of gold coins as well, and give me the coat!'

Aldar Kose finally agreed, and climbed down from his poor old horse.

He removed his coat and hat, and quickly put on those of the Bai, which quickly warmed him through.

He took hold of the heavy purse of gold coins, and climbed onto the Bai's magnificent horse.

As Aldar Kose rode away, he looked back to see the Bai standing in the deep snow, pulling on the old coat with seventy holes.

The Bai looked confused.

'I've just remembered my father's warning about the coat,' called Aldar Kose as he rode off.

'The magic only works for me.'

Freeze!

A telling technique

A tableau is a 'still image' made by one or more students, and it is a powerfully physical way to represent a moment in a story; it is often a starting point for improvised drama.

Dongguo and the Wolf is a Chinese folk tale first printed during the Ming Dynasty in 1544, and it was beautifully told to me by Ren Yubo, a student who also goes by the name of Ryan.

To rehearse, pay particular attention to mimed actions – such as removing the arrow from the wolf's wound, opening the bag, tying the wolf inside and putting the heavy bag across your shoulder. This makes the story easier to understand, as well as more engaging.

Before telling

Say: *If your **friend** is in trouble, you'll help. But if your **enemy** is in trouble, and only you can help, what will you do?*

Let the students listen to a few of each other's ideas. If they need more prompting, ask them to consider what they would do if they saw the local bully drowning in a river.

While telling

There is plenty of opportunity to get the students interacting in role towards the end of this tale. Pause when the farmer asks Dongguo *What will you do?* – as if *you* are the old farmer and *they* are Dongguo – perhaps reminding them about Dongguo's kind heart.

Listen to several different suggestions before you carry on to the end.

After telling

Ask the students to make three different tableaux from the story – the first two individually:

1 *Stand up, and show me a still image of Dongguo when you see the wounded wolf for the first time. Your bag is on your back and your donkey is behind you. Remember: Dongguo has a kind heart – you are afraid of the wolf, but you also feel pity for the wolf …*
3–2–1 Freeze!
Now relax. You're going to show me that still image again, but make it clearer and stronger. Use your knees, your shoulders, your hands, your eyes …
3–2–1 Freeze!
2 *Now show me the wolf, just after you have been freed from the bag and you're preparing to devour Dongguo. Make a strong still image …*
3–2–1 Freeze!

3 *Now stand in a group of three. One of you is the old farmer arriving with your hoe across your shoulder. One of you is the wolf who is so hungry and desperate to eat Dongguo. One of you is Dongguo and it's your last chance. Make a still image. 3–2–1 Freeze!*
Keep that still image, and when I say 'Action!' you're going to act out that scene with words, using your hands, your faces, your bodies. Get ready to bring the scene to life …
3–2–1 Action!

After the students have played the scene once, say: *Do the scene again. This time, you know what you're going to say, so focus on listening to each other and taking turns to speak. Make sure your voices, your expressions and your actions are clear. Make your starting image again …*
3–2–1 Action!

Invite a group who acts out the scene well to show it to the class. Before they start, ask the other students to notice what works particularly well in the group's performance, and to be ready to tell them at the end. This will focus the listeners' attention, and the feedback at the end will give confidence to the three performers – and to the whole class.

To follow on, take the opportunity offered by the dilemma in this story to further discuss the following questions about the ethics of helping an enemy, first in groups and then as a class:
Should Dongguo help and trust the wolf?
Think of someone who has harmed you – would you help them if they were in trouble?

Dongguo and the Wolf
A Chinese folk tale

There was once a generous man called Dongguo who travelled with his donkey. So kindhearted was he, that he led the donkey by a rope and carried the load himself so as not to burden the animal.

One day, as he walked through the forest, a wolf appeared suddenly from between the trees. The wolf had an arrow in its side.

'Help me. I have been shot by the hunter and he will surely kill me.'

Dongguo took pity on the wolf but said, 'If I come close to you, you will surely devour me. You are a man-eating wolf.'

'I am a wolf, but I am not a man-eater. Please help me,' cried the wolf.

Dongguo and the Wolf

Dongguo came up to the wolf, and gently drew the arrow from the poor wolf's side. Then he took his bag from his back and opened it up so that the wolf could crawl inside. The great beast filled the bag and Dongguo tied it closed.

He heaved the heavy bag onto his back and walked on, with the donkey following.

Soon the hunter appeared from between the trees.

'I am tracking a wolf I shot with an arrow. Has it come past you?'
'No wolf has come past me,' answered Dongguo.

The hunter went on between the trees. When he was out of sight, Dongguo lifted the heavy bag down from his back and opened it to release the wolf.

The wolf turned to Dongguo:
'Thank you for saving me. Now I am hungry. Which shall I eat first, you or the donkey?'

At that, the frightened donkey broke free and ran as fast as it could away into the forest, braying loudly.

Dongguo said, 'What are you saying? You are not a man-eating wolf and I saved your life.'

'Have you ever heard of a wolf that does not eat man? I am a wolf. It is my nature to eat man.'

'I ask for justice,' said Dongguo, 'for it is written that a man may seek judgements from three ancient ones.'

The hungry wolf agreed. After all, it would be easy to catch Dongguo, whatever judgements were given.

In the forest stood an ancient peach tree.

Dongguo told the peach tree:

'I seek justice. I saved the wolf from the hunter, and now the wolf intends to devour me. Give your judgement.'

The peach tree spoke:
'When I was younger, many sweet and delicious peaches hung from my branches and I gave them freely to man, who picked and ate them all. Now I am old, no more peaches grow. Man will come and cut me down, chop me into firewood and burn me. I judge that the wolf may devour you.'

Along came an ancient water buffalo.

Dongguo told the water buffalo:

'I seek justice. I saved the wolf from the hunter, and now the wolf intends to devour me. Give your judgement.'

The water buffalo spoke:
'When I was young, I worked hard for man to plough his fields so he could grow rice. I gave my labour freely. Now I am old, I am no longer strong enough to pull the plough. Man will slaughter me and eat my meat. I judge that the wolf may devour you.'

By now, the wolf was so hungry that he could barely stop himself from jumping on Dongguo, but Dongguo said:
'I may seek one more judgement.'

At that moment an old farmer appeared, carrying a hoe across his shoulder.

Dongguo told the farmer:

'I seek justice. I saved the wolf from the hunter, and now the wolf intends to devour me.'

'Tell me what happened.'
'The wolf was shot by the hunter, and I took the arrow from its side and hid the wolf in my bag.'
'Impossible!' cried the farmer. 'How can a great wolf fit inside such a small bag?'

'This is what happened,' said Dongguo.
'I cannot imagine this great beast inside this small bag.'

The wolf was desperate to eat Dongguo.

'It is true,' said the wolf. 'Now make your judgement.'

'I cannot make my judgement until I see the wolf inside the bag with my own eyes.'

The farmer held the bag open, and the impatient and hungry wolf climbed inside.

Quickly, the farmer tied the bag closed and turned to Dongguo:
'Now the wolf is inside the bag, what will you do?'

Kindhearted Dongguo once again felt pity for the wolf. He did not answer.

Without waiting, the farmer took his hoe and beat the wolf until it was dead.

The farmer said to Dongguo:
'It is the wolf's nature to eat man. Do not trust your enemy.'

Act it out!

A telling technique

Acting out a story through roleplay develops a greater understanding of characters' viewpoints, and students can explore the story by experiencing it 'from the inside'.

The Coat is a simple and yet profound Jewish folk tale that I learnt from Israeli storyteller Hanna Jaffe at a Storytelling for Peace event, where she performed together with a Palestinian Muslim storyteller.

To rehearse, practise miming actions – such as digging, chopping wood, warming yourself in front of a small fire – and find distinct voices for each of the three characters.

Before telling

Ask the students to tell a partner about an occasion when they felt extremely cold. They should describe:
- The time
- The place
- The cause of their coldness
- Who they were with
- Their feelings
- What they did
- How long they were cold for
- What happened in the end

While telling

Your clearly-mimed actions and distinct character voices will help the students to remember and act out the story afterwards.

After telling

Get the students to stand in groups of three, and make sure each group has a piece of fabric or clothing that can represent the coat.

Say: *It's the first visit to the wise one:*
- *One of you is the old father.*
- *One is the son.*
- *One is the wise one.*

The father and son are each holding a sleeve of the coat. You're about to knock on the wise one's door. The wise one is going to want to know the reasons why each of you believes you should have the coat, before deciding what to do. Make a still image – find the way this weak old person, this strong young person and this wise person all stand. Be careful with the coat – remember: it's very special to you.
Get ready …
3–2–1 Action!

Invite one or two groups to show their scene to the class.

Now say: *Find your own space in the room, alone. You are still the same character in the story.*
- *Old person, you are in front of the tiny fire trying to stay warm, but you can't.*
- *Young person, you are working in the freezing cold fields trying to keep warm, but you can't.*
- *Wise one, you are at home, you have the coat, and you are warm enough.*

I'm going to ask your character three questions. You can all whisper your answers to yourselves at the same time.
- *What happened before, and how did it make you feel?*
  (Allow time for most students to finish before asking …)
- *How are you feeling, and what are you thinking now?*
  (And when the students are ready …)
- *Who needs the coat more than you, and why?*

Invite one old parent, one young person and one wise one to each say part of their whispered monologue out loud, for the class to listen to.

Say: *Stand in your groups of three again. It's the second visit to the wise one in the story. You're about to knock on the wise one's door again. The wise one is going to want to know the reasons why each of you believes the other one should have the coat before deciding what to do. Make a still image and find your body posture …*
3–2–1 Action!

Again, invite one or two groups to show their scene to the class.

To follow on, ask small groups of students to talk about situations which *The Coat* reminds them of in their own personal experience, or on a national or international scale. Each small-group discussion can lead to a piece of writing:
- It could be an account of a real-life act of selfishness or unselfishness.
- It could be a believable piece of *creative* writing based on a real-life event.

Once complete, the students from different groups can read each other's work and guess how much truth there is in each of the other students' narratives.

The Coat

A Jewish folk tale

There were once a father and son who were so poor that, between them, they had just one coat.

'I should have the coat,' said the old father. 'All day long, I sit in the cold house before the tiny fire trying to keep warm.'

'I should have the coat,' said the son. 'All day long, I work outside in the cold wind. You have the fire to keep you warm.'

'But I'm too old to work. Digging in the fields and chopping wood should keep you warm.'

The father and son argued and argued and never agreed, so they went to the wise man.

Each of them said why he should have the coat.

'You both want to keep the coat,' said the wise man. 'Go away and leave the coat with me.'

The father returned to the house, and the son returned to the fields.

The father thought about his son working without a coat in the cold wind.

The son thought about his father sitting before the tiny fire in the cold house.

'You should have the coat,' said the father at the end of the day, 'for your need is greater than mine.'

'You should have the coat,' said the son, 'for you need it more than me.'

The next day, they both went to the wise man. Each said why the other should have the coat.

'Here is the coat,' said the wise man. 'Before, each of you wanted to keep the coat for himself, so I wanted to keep the coat for myself. Now, both of you want to give, so now I want to give as well. Take the coat and, here, take my coat as well.'

Responding in role

A telling technique

The students can explore the inner world of a character by being interviewed in role at a particular moment in the story, after they have heard it.

Garuda and Turtle is a story I was told by a Thai student many years ago, and I've been telling it ever since.

To rehearse this tale, bear in mind that its simplicity is part of its beauty. So it makes sense to tell it in simple language and with a simple repeated rhyme.

Before telling

Tell the students that you are going to tell a story told in Thailand about Garuda, the sacred bird of the gods.

While telling

Encourage the students to repeat the rhyme 'If you beat me, you can eat me' and the response 'Just ahead of you, Garuda' along with you. Pause just before the end – when you ask How did Turtle beat Garuda? – for the students to come up with ideas, before you finish the story.

After telling

In a calm voice, say: Close your eyes and sit quietly. Imagine Garuda at one moment in the story, frozen in time.
- Notice the exact position of his body, his wings and the angle of his head … Step up close, and have a closer look at his eyes and beak … Remember what you see.
- Imagine moving slowly around Garuda … Look from each side … Notice his size, the colours in his feathers and the look in his eyes … Can you imagine his smell?
- Now get ready to reach out and touch Garuda on his back … Notice how he feels: rough or smooth; hot or cold; strong or weak; calm or tense; happy or sad … What do you feel as you run your hand up his back and along his wings? … Feel his neck, the shape of his head … Feel his beak if you want to … Now take your hand away.
- Stand back and watch, as this moment in the story comes to life … What movements are there? What sounds are there? Listen closely … You are right there in the story …

Now let this moment be strong in your memory so you can remember everything, and slowly come back to this room. You can open your eyes and sit quietly.

During this guided mental imagery exercise, some students will appear more focused than others, but it is hard to know what is going on inside their heads.

Now gently interview a volunteer student, inviting them to close their eyes before you begin. Make it clear that they don't have to answer all of the questions you ask.

Ask questions such as the ones below, but let your questions be led by the answers the student gives:
- Which moment in the story are you imagining?
  What do you notice about the landscape and the sky?
  What do you notice about Garuda?
  Tell me more about that.
  How do you feel as you step close to him?
  What do you notice when you move around Garuda?
  How do you feel about touching him?
  What do you notice?
  Tell me more about that.
  What else do you see … smell … feel … hear?
- Now **you are** Garuda at this moment in the story:
  How do you feel?
  Tell me about how you feel about Turtle.
  Why are you acting in this way?
  What do you want?

Now invite another student to be interviewed – with their eyes closed. This time, the other students can ask the questions – following your model:
- Firstly, the interviewee is an observer describing Garuda from the outside.
- Secondly, the interviewee steps into the role of Garuda.

Be ready to paraphrase any questions that are unclear or inappropriate. Encourage the students to listen for subtle differences between this student's answers and the answers of the previous student.
- Some other students may be happy to describe a moment from the story – put them in small groups with others who can interview them.
- Some students might prefer to be interviewed as Turtle.

To follow on, ask the students to talk about how they interpret the meaning of the story.
- Some may talk about power struggles, others may talk about using intelligence or imagination to get out of difficulties, while others may talk about the effectiveness of cooperation.
- These different personal interpretations can be discussed, first in groups and then as a whole class, and the students can be encouraged to notice the different ways of understanding the story.

They might compare this tale with equivalent tales they know from other cultures, such as The Hare and the Tortoise – an Aesop fable which is told around the world.

The students could also look at images of Garuda and read about this sacred bird in Buddhist mythology and among Hindu deities (see Google Images and Wikipedia).

Garuda and Turtle

A tale from Thailand

Garuda, the bird of the gods, flew with power and speed.

He flew down from the mountain of the gods, and a wind blew across the land below as his wings beat the air. He shone so brightly that none could look at him.

Garuda flew down towards the great swamp where Turtle was slowly swimming, took Turtle in his powerful beak and was about to swallow, when Turtle cried:

'I am too small a creature for you to eat, Great Garuda, let me go.'

Garuda paid no attention to Turtle.

'Let me go, and I will beat you in a race across the swamp. If you beat me, you can eat me.'

Now Garuda began to pay attention to Turtle. He opened his beak, allowing Turtle to drop back down into the swamp.

'I am Garuda, the fastest and most powerful of all. How could a small, slow creature like you beat me?'

'I will prove it. Be here tomorrow at sunrise, and I will race you in any direction across the swamp. If you beat me, you can eat me.'

Proud Garuda laughed at the small turtle and flew into the sky, the sun reflected in his long and powerful wings.

'Until sunrise,' he called.

At sunrise the next morning, Garuda returned to find Turtle waiting.

'I am Garuda, the fastest and most powerful of all. How could a small, slow creature like you beat me? I will eat you now.'

'If you beat me, you can eat me. In which direction shall we race across the swamp, Great Garuda?'

'Towards the East, the rising sun.'

Garuda flew calmly towards the East, his wings magnificent in the rising sun.

After a short while, he called down: 'Turtle, Turtle!'

'Just ahead of you, Garuda,' came the answer from the swamp below.

Garuda was amazed and changed his course, flying towards the South. He beat his wings and flew faster over the swamp.

After some time, he called down: 'Turtle, Turtle!'

'Just ahead of you, Garuda,' came the answer from the swamp below.

Garuda could not understand. He turned sharply towards the East and flew with such power and speed that a great wind blew across the swamp.

After a long time flying, he was becoming tired. He called down: 'Turtle, Turtle!'

'Just ahead of you, Garuda,' came the answer from the swamp below.

Now Garuda was afraid. How could a small creature like Turtle make the Great Garuda look so foolish?

Summoning the last of his energy, Garuda beat his wings hard and soared at lightning speed toward the North.

But after many hours flying, Garuda became so exhausted that he only just managed to call down: 'Turtle, Turtle!'

'Just ahead of you, Garuda,' came the answer from the swamp below.

Garuda had lost the race.

Ashamed, he flew on and on, returning to Sumeru, the sacred mountain of the gods.

But, I ask you, how did Turtle beat Garuda?

In the great swamps of Thailand, there swim a great many turtles and, in that night, a message had been passed on from one to another, all across that great community, so that every turtle knew how to answer the call of Great Garuda.

Responding with a task

A telling technique

Rather than having to talk about a story straight away, the students can be given the opportunity to choose their mode of expression after listening – to write or draw what they imagined.

The Snowgirl is a folk tale I heard from a Russian student during an intercultural evening at Exeter University. Her enchanting storytelling transported us all to her homeland in the Urals.

To rehearse, keep the language you use clear and simple – this will make it easy for the students to create their own mental images.

Before telling

Tell the students that this tale comes from the Urals, a remote region of Central Russia, where traditional stories are closely linked to nature, and the Earth itself is alive and breathing.

While telling

Imagine the landscape and the snowgirl as you tell the story, but *describe* only a few details. This will leave space for the students to create their own mental images of the landscape and the snowgirl.

After telling

Tell the students that you are going to ask some questions, and that they are going to answer them *silently* – in their imaginations. Make sure each student has a blank piece of paper ready to write or draw on afterwards.

Invite them to close their eyes if they wish. Say:
Step into the story of the snowgirl. Find one moment in the story and make it still … Imagine your answers to these questions:

- *Look at this moment in the story. Where are you standing, where are you looking at this picture from? … Step closer and let the picture become clearer … Look at the whole picture … What do you see? What colours, what shapes?*
- *Can you feel the temperature at this moment in the story?*
- *Choose one sound that you can hear at this moment in the story … Where is the sound coming from? How does the sound make you feel?*
- *There's a smell, perhaps it's not a strong smell, but can you imagine a smell at this moment in the story? … What is it? How does the smell make you feel?*
- *Choose and imagine one person in this moment … Reach out and touch this person on the shoulders … You can feel what this person is feeling …*

Keep all these images in your head and, when you're ready, look at me … I'll give each of you a choice: Speak and listen to a partner. Alternatively, write or draw (or write and draw) on paper.

- The speakers/listeners get into pairs to describe their chosen moments to each other in detail. As they listen, they can ask for more detail. They can then change partners with other speakers/listeners and find out about a new partner's 'moment'.
- The writers/drawers work alone on their paper.

When everyone is ready, the writers/drawers make new small groups with speakers/listeners, to show and/or talk about what they have done on paper. They can answer questions about what they have written and/or drawn.

Now that the whole class has described a moment from the story, ask the students to stand in a circle in the order that their moment occurs in the story. It is likely that there will be more than one student with the same moment – these students stand next to each other.

The story is retold, with each student briefly presenting *their* moment.

- The speakers describe their moment.
- The writers may read aloud or talk about what they wrote.
- The drawers can display and/or describe their pictures.

To follow on, remind everyone that, at the end of the story, the snowgirl comes to her mother in a dream, which has a profound effect on the mother.

- The students imagine that a few winters have passed and they are going to send a message to the snowgirl, either from the mother or the father – or someone else in the community.
- The message can be a song, a poem, a letter, a piece of artwork, a dance – or anything else.

The students work alone or in pairs to prepare their message, and then present them in turn.

The Snowgirl

A tale from Russia

Once long ago, in a village in the Urals of Russia, there lived an old woman with her old husband. She had everything she needed: a good marriage, a good home, a good community.

But not quite everything.

She didn't have a child. She had no daughter. Oh, how she wished for a daughter.

'Husband, do you think we shall ever have a daughter?' 'Wife, it is too late, we are too old.'

Winter came.

The snow began to fall thick and fast, blanketing the ground so all was white. On midwinter's eve, the old woman went out of the house into the snow-bright darkness.

As if in a dream, she worked in the snow with her clever hands until she had made a beautiful snowgirl.

The old woman went into the house and went to bed.

In the morning she awoke to the sound of laughter, light and happy. She went to the window and saw, running and skipping and playing in the snow, the snowgirl.

The old woman went to the door, and the snowgirl ran towards her and threw herself into her mother's arms, laughing with joy.

How the old woman loved her daughter, the snowgirl, so full of life and love.

The old woman showed her new daughter to her husband, and he loved the snowgirl too. They were a family.

Soon the snowgirl knew the other children of the community, and everyone loved her.

Every day, she played in the snow, running, dancing and leaping lightly into the air.

The months passed, and the woman forgot the time before the snowgirl came. It was as if she had always had a daughter.

The snow still lay deep on the ground.

Finally there was a slight warmth in the air, and the snow began to melt.

It was time for the festival to mark the end of winter and to welcome new life.

A great fire was built and all the community gathered around the fire and sang to celebrate the coming of spring.

The snowgirl stood with her mother.

One of the children ran forward and leapt through the flames, then another child, and another. As they jumped over the fire, they shouted out with joy.

Soon every child had leapt over the fire, every child – except the snowgirl.

It was her turn, but she hid in her mother's skirts.

'Go, my child, do as the other children do.'

The snowgirl looked up at her mother, her eyes wide and shining.

'Go, my daughter, jump through the flames.'

The girl began to run, light-footed, towards the fire. She looked back once at her mother, and smiled.

And then she leapt high into the air above the hot flames – and was gone.

The whole community fell silent. One by one, they turned and walked back to their homes.

But the old woman stood until the sky was dark and the fire was dead.

Her heart was broken.

She went back to her home and she cried. Her husband tried to comfort her but she turned away from him. There she stayed, in her home, never going out into the sunshine.

The spring passed, the summer passed, the autumn passed, and the old woman cried for the daughter she had lost.

Winter finally came, and the snow began to fall. One night, the old woman had a dream. In her dream, the snowgirl came to her.

'Cry for me no longer, mother. No more tears. Mother, I am with you. When the snow falls, I am the snow. When you wash clothes in the river, I am the water. I am the water you drink from the well. I am always with you.'

When she awoke, the woman was no longer sad. Every day, she celebrated the life of her daughter, the snowgirl.

She would always be with her.

Responding with a gift

A telling technique

The students choose a gift they would give to a character in a story, and compare their ideas.

Mbongoro is a Shona tale I learnt from Tawanda Nhire Nelson Antonio, who teaches English in Mozambique. When he told it to me at the 2010 IATEFL Conference, he asked me to pass it on. I've since told it to hundreds of students from around the world who are now telling it to others. This growing network is an example of direct transmission, the oldest way of passing on a story orally.

To rehearse, focus carefully on the rhythmic repetition of *'Could he/they find the donkey?'* and *'Mbongoro'*, which is an old word for 'Donkey' in Shona. Personally, I love to accompany this tale with percussion – either a shaker or a drum. You could try this yourself, or ask a student with a good sense of rhythm to accompany you.

You can find another creative way of telling this folk tale in *Imagine That!* by Jane Arnold, Herbert Puchta and Mario Rinvolucri (Helbling Languages 2007).

Before telling

Explain to the students the origin of this story and that, if they listen closely and then tell it to others, *they* can become part of this worldwide network, too.

In many cultures, a short 'call and response' is customary before starting a story – this acts as a kind of 'contract' between listeners and storyteller: that they will be *part of* the story. In Shona:

- The storyteller calls: *Kwaivepo* – /kwaˈjivepo/ – meaning 'Long ago'.
- The listeners respond: *Zepfunde* – /zepˈfundei/ – meaning 'We are into the story'.

Before I tell *Mbongoro*, we all chant this call and response three times, each time with greater energy and volume than the time before – and then launch into the story itself.

See page 37 for more on 'opening' and 'call and response' techniques.

While telling

Pause briefly after saying *'the workers fetched their spades from the fields'*, and allow a moment for the students to imagine what the farmer is going to do.

It is not necessary for the students to say what they imagine, as this might break up the rhythm of the storytelling.

After telling

Ask the students: *What did you think of the farmer's idea to bury the donkey alive?*

Give them time to briefly discuss their answers in pairs:
- Some might say that he is clever and knew that the donkey would get out.
- Others will say he is cruel.

Say: *It is the end of the story. The farmer, the donkey keeper, the fieldworkers and the donkey are all there.*
- *Imagine you can give any gift to one of the characters. Think which character and which gift – perhaps you can describe the gift, or say why you're giving it.*
- *Imagine your partner is that character and give your partner the gift.*

When you are ready, you can begin.

When the students have exchanged their gifts, find out about some of them:
- Some may be highly practical, like a carrot for the donkey after such a long and hard task.
- Some may be symbolic, such as wings for the donkey.
- Some may be personal qualities, like humility for the farmer.
- Some may be skills, like the ability to speak for the donkey.

To follow on, ask the students to stand facing each other in pairs. Say:
- *One of you is a member of the community, but you don't know what happened at the water hole. You want to know everything that happened and how your partner felt about it.*
- *The other is one of the fieldworkers who dug the earth. You want to tell your partner everything that happened and find out what your partner thinks about what you say.*
  Get ready …
  3–2–1 Action!

They will find themselves retelling a large part of the story from their character's perspective, and may well make up new details. Invite one or two pairs to perform an extract from their conversation for the whole class.

Remind the students that *they* can become part of a worldwide 'direct transmission' storytelling network by passing this story on to others.

Mbongoro

A Shona tale from Zimbabwe

Once, there was a farmer who had a donkey, not a beautiful donkey but an old donkey, called Mbongoro.

The donkey was looked after by a donkey-keeper who fed the donkey, watered the donkey and groomed the donkey.

One day, the donkey-keeper found the donkey had broken its rope and run away.

He went looking for the donkey, calling 'Mbongoro, Mbongoro, Mbongoro'.

But could he find the donkey?
No.

He came to the workers digging in the fields.

'The farmer's donkey has run away. Help me to find him.'

So together they went through the fields, calling 'Mbongoro, Mbongoro, Mbongoro'.

But could they find the donkey?
No.

'Go back and tell the farmer,' the workers told the donkey-keeper.

So he went and knocked at the farmer's door.

'That foolish old donkey! We'll find him together.'

So the farmer, the donkey-keeper and the fieldworkers went looking for the donkey, calling 'Mbongoro, Mbongoro, Mbongoro'.

And could they find the donkey?
Yes, they could.

They listened, and heard the donkey braying. They found the donkey stuck in a waterhole he had fallen into when he ran away during the night.

It was a small hole:
It was as long as the donkey was, from the tip of his nose to the end of his tail.
It was as wide as the donkey was, from one side to the other.
It was as deep as the donkey was, from the tips of his ears to his hooves.

'Get out, you foolish old Mbongoro!' shouted the farmer, but the donkey just looked up at him.

The donkey was stuck tight.

'Pull the donkey out!' shouted the farmer.

The workers reached down and took hold of the donkey's hair in their hands and pulled. Poor donkey!

The donkey was stuck tight.

'Fetch a rope!' shouted the farmer.

The donkey-keeper fetched a rope, but he couldn't get it around the donkey.

The donkey was stuck tight.

'Go and fetch your spades from the fields!' shouted the farmer.

The workers fetched their spades from the fields.

'There's nothing for it. Bury that foolish old donkey alive!' shouted the farmer.

'Bury the donkey alive?'
'Bury my foolish old donkey alive!'

The workers had no choice. They dug with their spades, and threw the soft earth onto the donkey's back. With the earth on his back, the old donkey began to shake. The earth trickled down the donkey's sides and into the hole.

The workers continued to dig.

With more earth on his back, the donkey shook again and the earth trickled down into the hole.

Now the donkey began to tread with his hooves, pressing the wet earth into the bottom of the waterhole.

As the workers dug, they called:

'Mbongoro, Mbongoro, Mbongoro. Shake! Shake! Mbongoro, Mbongoro, Mbongoro. Shake! Shake!'

Slowly the donkey rose up, up and up, and finally stepped out of the hole.

The workers looked at the donkey, and the workers looked at the farmer, and they wondered:

Which one was the old fool?

Responding personally

A telling technique

The students give their personal responses to questions they choose personally from a list, and find out how differently others interpreted the same story.

The Fly is a tale with enchanting riddles, which inspired me to start telling it myself. I came across the story in *Favorite Folktales from Around the World* by Jane Yolen (Pantheon 1986). She in turn found it in *The Toad is the Emperor's Uncle: Animal Tales from Vietnam* (Doubleday 1970).

To rehearse, practise miming the actions with conviction – such as pointing to the fly on the wall and, later, pointing to the fly on the moneylender's nose. This will bring the tale to life and help the students follow the plot.

Practise pausing and gesturing – to invite the students to join in with the mysterious, repeated riddles – *'selling the wind to buy the moon'* and *'cutting down living trees to plant dead ones'.*

Before telling

Encourage a student to promise to do something in the next lesson, such as sing a song, tell a story or recite a poem, and elicit from the others that they are witnesses to this promise.

- This will introduce the notion of the witness – which is key to this story.
- Of course, the witnesses need to make sure that the promise is kept!

While telling

Pause at the end, before the boy speaks to the judge, and let the students guess what the boy might say.

After telling

Give out or display a long list of questions like the ones opposite:

- The students quickly select about five they would like to respond to.
- In groups of three, each student responds to *their own* questions, and listens to the others responding to the questions *they* chose.

Remind them that there are no 'correct' answers to these questions, and encourage them to listen carefully to and remember their partners' ideas.

To follow on, each student can write down, edit and redraft some of their responses in *written* form. Alternatively, they can represent their ideas as *artwork*. Their work can be compiled as a book or a classroom wall display.

- Which character made a strong impression on you?
- Who enjoyed the story in this class?
- Who in your family might enjoy this story?
- What was the strongest image in your mind during the story?
- What colour was the story?
- What kind of settings did you imagine?
- Can you describe what one of the characters looked like in your imagination?
- What sounds did you imagine during the story?
- What was your strongest feeling during the story?
- What surprised you in the story?
- What upset you in the story?
- What made you laugh?
- What did the story mean to you personally?
- What did you like best in the story?
- What didn't you like in the story?
- What did you notice about the storyteller's voice?
- Did the storyteller like the story?
- What thoughts went through your head during the story?
- Was listening to the story like being in a dream?
- Which character in the story were you?
- Which part of the story would you like to hear again?
- How did the story begin?
- How did you think the story was going to end?
- Did you want to join in with the storytelling?
- How long did it take to tell this story?
- Is it a children's story?
- What is the most senseless question in this list?
- What question is missing from this list?

The Fly

A Vietnamese folk tale

There once lived a rich and powerful moneylender.

One day, he came to the small house of a poor family to collect the money they owed him.

He banged on the door for a long time until a boy answered.

'Are your father and mother at home?'

The boy shook his head, but the moneylender did not believe him.

'It is time for them to pay me the debt they owe me. Let me in.'

The moneylender pushed his way past the boy, and saw that indeed he was alone in the small house.

'Where are your mother and father?'
'My father is cutting down living trees to plant dead ones. My mother is selling the wind to buy the moon.'

'Foolish child! Tell me where your father and mother are!'
'My father is cutting down living trees to plant dead ones. My mother is selling the wind to buy the moon.'

The moneylender was furious.
'I must know where they are!'

The moneylender looked around again, to make sure no one else was there.

'Tell me where they are and I will cancel their debt.'

'How can I believe you?' said the boy. 'There is no witness here.'
'The walls of the house are witness.'
'The walls cannot be witness. The walls are not living.'

'See the fly sitting on the wall there? That fly is living. Now tell me where your father and mother are and they will owe me nothing.'

The boy looked carefully at the fly on the wall, and then nodded in agreement.

'My father is cutting down living trees to plant dead ones – he is cutting lengths of bamboo and putting them into the ground to build a fence.
My mother is selling the wind to buy the moon – she is at the market selling fans so that she can buy oil to light our lamp at night.'

The moneylender laughed to himself and left the house.

That night, he returned to the small house and banged on the door.

The father and mother let him in and he demanded that they pay their debt. They pleaded with him because they had no money to pay, and the moneylender was furious.

The boy, woken by the noise, said:
'My father and mother owe you nothing because you cancelled the debt.'

The moneylender laughed: 'Who would believe a boy?'

The next day, the matter was brought before the judge.

The rich and powerful moneylender said:
'Their debt is overdue and they will not pay. I demand payment immediately.'

The boy stepped forward:
'The moneylender came to our house in the day and he promised me that the debt was cancelled.'

'Nonsense,' shouted the moneylender. 'I did not go to the house in the day. And I certainly made no such promise. Who would believe a boy? Where is the witness?'

'The witness was a fly.'

'A fly?' said the judge, 'How can a fly be a witness?'
'Yes, the witness was a fly, and it was sitting right there on the end of the moneylender's nose.'

The moneylender was furious:
'The fly was not sitting on the end of my nose! The fly was sitting on the wall!'

For a moment there was silence in the courtroom, and then everyone began to laugh, even the judge.

The only one who didn't laugh was the rich and powerful moneylender, because everyone was laughing at him.

The poor family's debt was cancelled.

Exploring metaphor

A telling technique

It is useful to provide students with a clear framework – such as a matching activity – so that they can use metaphors to express their ideas about how a story relates to their own experience.

The Snake Wife was told in one of my classes by a young Korean adult called Dong. I remember the powerful impact his storytelling had on the students.

To rehearse this tale, keep it simple so that the students can interpret the powerful metaphors it contains. Find a distinct voice for the snake wife. You could also look for a resonant bell – to ring twice at the appropriate moment.

Before telling

Ask the class: *If someone is unsure what to do next in their life, what can they do?* The students listen to a few different ideas from each other. These might include: asking for advice, going on a journey, trying a new activity, a prayer or a meditation.

While telling

Pause briefly after saying *'The young man prepared to die'* in order to add suspense, and again after *'How could the bell have sounded?'* – to give the students a moment to ponder.

After telling

Say: *Choose a moment in the story, and hold a still image of that moment in your mind. See it. Feel it. Hear it. Now spend a couple of minutes drawing or writing (or drawing and writing) about that moment on a piece of paper.*

As each student finishes, invite them to stand and make pairs with others who have finished, and to find out about the image *they* imagined and described. It is for the students to decide:
- They can *talk* about their writing or drawing.
- They can *show* it to each other.

Early finishers might talk to five or six different partners, while late finishers might just talk to two or three.

Make sure each student has five pieces of A5 paper, and ask them to write each of the five characters in the story:
- Student
- Snake husband
- Snake wife
- Young bird
- Parent birds

They should write each of the characters in the middle of a different piece of paper.

Now dictate or write on the board the concept nouns below in pairs of opposites.

honesty	*deceit*
bravery	*cowardice*
intelligence	*foolishness*
innocence	*slyness*
freedom	*captivity*
kindness	*cruelty*
independence	*dependence*
selflessness	*selfishness*
hope	*despair*

Working alone, the students write some (not all) of these words around different characters on the separate pieces of paper.
- They prepare to say *why* they have chosen each noun.
- They prepare to say *which point* in the story they are thinking of.

(There are no right or wrong answers.)

After a few minutes, the whole class listens while a volunteer student talks to you about one of the nouns they have chosen. *Your* role is just to understand their response to the story – not to evaluate what they say.

Ask the students to sit in circles of three or four and to listen to each other's interpretations.

Remind them that when they listen to stories, they all find their own meanings – the characters and events are metaphors for aspects of their lives. The meanings and metaphors they find depend on culture, background, temperament and personal experience.
- They should listen for similarities and differences between the ways they understand the story of the snake wife.
- They should remember the *differences*, especially, so that they are ready to talk about them together afterwards.

When the groups have had enough time, bring the whole class together to talk about the differences in their interpretations of *The Snake Wife*.

To follow on, the students can write freely about the story, and what it means to them – with regard to their own lives.

This writing can be redrafted and presented as a wall display or a class book.

The Snake Wife

A Korean tale

A student left his family and set off to make his way in the world.

He went up the mountain looking for self-knowledge because he knew that, at the top, was a sacred bell.

Perhaps when he heard the sound of the bell, he would find direction in his life.

As he reached the end of his long and tiring climb, he noticed a young fledgling bird caught in the mouth of a long and powerful snake.

The student picked up the nearest rock and threw it hard at the snake. The snake was killed and the young bird was free to fly away.

The student continued to climb, but night was falling. He was surprised to find a house ahead of him on the path.

A beautiful woman with smooth skin stepped out of the house and invited him in to eat and rest.

After a delicious meal, the young man was shown to his bed.

In the middle of the night, he felt something pressing down on his chest. He couldn't breathe. He opened his eyes to find a snake coiled around his body, squeezing the air from him.

'Help me!' he cried out.

The snake answered, 'You killed my husband with a rock, and now I will take your life.'

Tighter and tighter the snake wife coiled herself around the student, until he felt the life being squeezed out of him.

'Please let me go!' he begged.

The snake wife laughed:
'I will free you if you can make the sacred bell sound twice.'

'How can I do this when you have me here trapped?'

The student struggled but there was nothing he could do.

The young man prepared to die.

At that moment, he heard the sound of the sacred bell. It rang twice:

'Dong! Dong!'

The snake wife hissed in fury and uncoiled herself.

The scholar found himself upon the path, with no sign of the house or the snake.

How could the bell have sounded?

He rose to his feet, and managed to make his way up to the top of the mountain.

On the ground beneath the sacred bell were the bodies of two adult birds.

He looked up, and saw the young bird he had saved, flying away into the distance.

Exploring mental imagery

A telling technique

The students can be encouraged to explore and compare the visual, auditory and kinaesthetic imagery they notice when being told a story.

After the Fire is an extraordinarily powerful story from the Yucararé people of Bolivia – I found it on the wonderful Stories To Grow By website: www.storiestogrowby.com/stories/after_fire_bolivia.html

To rehearse, pay attention to the sensory description in this tale:

- Visual images, such as the land covered in ash.
- Auditory images, such as the voice of Sararuma the Sorcerer.
- Kinaesthetic images, such as the shrinking of Sararuma, and the green shoots of grass reaching for the sun.

Before telling

You can show the students a map of South America and let them know that the story comes from the Yucararé, indigenous people who live in the Bolivian lowlands of the Amazon Basin.

While telling

Because of the rich multi-sensory description in this story, you might not invite the students to join in as much as in other stories. Instead, allow them to immerse themselves in their imaginations.

After telling

In a slow and gentle voice, say:

- *Sit quietly and close your eyes. I'm going to ask some questions about the story, and I don't know what your answers will be. There are no right answers and no wrong answers. Whatever you imagine is perfect.*
- *Choose a moment from the story. Look at this moment in the story … Step a little closer, and let the picture become clear … What do you see exactly? How light or dark is it? What are the colours and the shapes … Now this picture is coming to life … What sounds are there? Listen closely … What movements are there?*
- *Now remember these three moments, and slowly come back to this room. You can open your eyes and sit quietly.*

Ask the students to talk in pairs and make a note of any details they imagined at that moment – for example, what exactly Sararuma the Sorcerer looks like, the sounds of the battle, how the man and woman dig themselves out from under the ground.

They can also note what they imagined at other moments during the story.

Divide the board into three sections:

- In the middle of the first section, write *Pictures*.
- In the other two, write *Sounds* and *Movements*.

Alternatively, make three large posters.

The students note down what they and their partners imagined in words and phrases. For example: *'Sararuma was floating a little above the ground'.*

They may need support to find ways of expressing what they imagined. This is an ideal learning opportunity for students who have something specific to say and need to find a way to express it.

Once their ideas have been displayed, ask them to talk in small groups about differences between what is written down and what they themselves imagined. This draws attention to how differently our imaginations work:

- Some might see animated cartoon images on a screen in their heads.
- Others might find themselves physically involved in the narrative, eg buried underground with the man and the woman in the darkness.

To follow on, say: *You could say that this Yucararé story is about hope, and you could say that this story is about lies. Explain to your partner which made a greater impression on you when you were listening: the lies or the hope?*

Ask the students to think about the consequences of Sararuma's lies. Then tell them about a lie you were once told, making sure you answer the questions below (that you will be asking the students as 'prompt' questions).

Choose carefully, taking your students into account – only do this next activity if you are confident that they will be comfortable.

Now say: *You can write about a lie that someone told you, but nobody else is going to read what you write.*

- *How did the lie make you feel?*
- *What happened as a result of the lie?*
- *Did you believe it?*
- *How did you find out that it was a lie?*
- *How do you feel when you remember that lie?*

After the students have finished their writing, ask them to put it away privately – although you could find out if there are any who would like to talk about their experience, and ask them to find a partner who they would like to tell.

After the Fire

A Bolivian tale

Long ago, on the high grasslands of Yuracaré in Bolivia, there lived two tribes; but there was drought, and both were suffering from hunger.

The evil sorcerer Sararuma appeared to the chief of one tribe:
'The other tribe are plotting to set fire to your land so that your people will die of hunger. Send your men to set fire to their land first.'

Sararuma, in his cloak of burning flames, now appeared to the chief of the other tribe:
'The other tribe are plotting to set fire to your land so that your people will die of hunger. Send your men to set fire to their land first.'

One man and one woman from one of the tribes went to their chief:
'Do not listen to Sararuma. His desire is for war and destruction. Do not attack, but speak words of peacemaking. On the land, both tribes can live.'

But the chief paid them no attention.

Soon the land was ablaze. Not only was the land burning, but the homes on both sides.

The people waged a terrible war, until all that remained upon the land was in flames.

Everyone was killed, and Sararuma grew huge. He flew across the land, his cloak ablaze, thrilled at the death and destruction he'd caused.

But the man and woman had buried themselves deep in the earth for safety and hid underground, waiting for the fire to pass. They could feel the heat of the flames and smell the smoke of the fire, even deep underground.

Many days passed, and the man dug at the earth above him with his hands and pushed a twig up through to the surface. The twig burst into flame.

'It is too soon. We must wait.'

Many more days passed, and the man dug at the earth above him with his hands and pushed a twig up through to the surface. The twig smouldered.

'It is too soon. We must wait longer.'

Many more days passed, and the man dug at the earth above him with his hands and pushed a twig up through to the surface.

The twig did not burn.

The man and the woman carefully dug above their heads for a long time until they reached the surface.

The land was grey with ash, the sky was grey with dust, there was no sign of life.

All was silent.

Suddenly Sararuma was before them, huge and powerful, his cloak burning so bright that they could not look.

His terrible laugh echoed across the deserted land:
'Why are you still here? There is nothing for you here. You will die like the others.'

The man said, 'We do not know what may happen. We don't have to die.'
The woman said, 'We will live.'

Sararuma became angry, no longer quite so big:
'Look around! There is no life, everything is dead. There is nothing to eat.'

In her closed hand, the woman felt the seeds that she had taken under the ground with her:
'Now the ground is dry, but soon we will plant.'

As she spoke, the blackened branches of the trees revealed green buds, and on the surface of the scorched earth appeared green shoots of grass.

Sararuma shrank still more until he was smaller than them, his cloak barely smouldering.

His voice was high and shrill:
'You are alone. There is no-one else. You will not survive.'

The man said:
'We cannot know what may happen, but we will go on.'

As he spoke, animals hiding underground began to nose their way out, searching for food. Birdsong could be heard far away.

The woman looked at the man and said:
'Things will change. We will have children.'

Sararuma diminished in size until he was as tiny as a child, and then smaller, until Sararuma became no more than a gust of wind, howling.

Exploring meaning

A telling technique

The students usually enjoy discussing the meanings in a folk tale, and how these meanings relate to their own experiences and values.

The Ferryman and the Grammar Teacher is my adaptation of another traditional Nasrudin Hodja short tale. This 'wise fool' (who also opened Chapter Two on page 70) features in thousands of tales – and there is always a punchline with a twist of wisdom at the end.

To rehearse, focus on the voice and posture of the pompous grammar teacher and the wise fool. Also practise the build-up of the storm – how to get the students to mime rowing on increasingly rough water with you, and to howl like the wind as you raise your voice.

Before telling

Ask the students for a list of the most important skills that a person needs to survive in the world, and write them up.
- Make sure 'Being able to swim' is included.
- Give pairs of students a minute to rank them.
- Where does 'Being able to swim' appear?

Now ask them to come up with a list of the most important skills a person needs to survive *in a foreign language*.
- Make sure 'Correct use of grammar' is included.
- Again, the students rank them.
- Where does 'Correct use of grammar' come?

While telling

This is a short joke tale, so enjoy the characters and the storm, and emphasise the punchline.

After telling

Tell the students to ask a partner: *What does this story mean?*

Invite the class to share ideas and discuss the different interpretations. Point out that many folk tales involve someone thinking they are superior, and then being punished for their arrogance.

Elicit situations in real life where one person might believe themselves to be superior to another, and write these situations up – two students just before an exam, two players during a game of golf, one neighbour showing off their expensively-renovated house …

The students discuss these in pairs and rehearse a short one-minute scene to act out, then think of things that might happen which make the superior 'show-off' individuals look really stupid.

Finally, they share their stories with the class.

To follow on, point out that this story seems to say that 'Correct use of grammar' is not important. This may be an ideal opportunity to start a discussion about when grammatical accuracy is less important than communicative competence, and when accuracy *is* important – for example, in most language tests.

The Ferryman and the Grammar Teacher

A tale from Turkey

Nasrudin Hodja was working as a ferryman, rowing people across the wide river in a small boat in exchange for payment.

One day, a grammar teacher came along.

'Will you carry me to the other side?'

'If you pay me.'

'Will the crossing be smooth or rough?' asked the grammar teacher.

'I don't know nothing.'

'*I don't know nothing?* Have you never learned grammar?'
'No, never.'
'Then you have wasted half of your life!'

Nasrudin Hodja began rowing the grammar teacher across the wide river.

Halfway across, the sky grew dark and the wind began to blow.

A storm broke; there was thunder and lightning.

The waves got bigger and bigger, and started crashing over the side of the small rowing boat.

The boat rocked from side to side – it was certain that the boat would be turned over.

Nasrudin looked at the grammar teacher who was holding on to the sides of the boat, terrified.

The colour had drained from his face.

Nasrudin called:

'Have you never learned to swim?'
'No. Never.'
'Then you have wasted all of your life!'

Chapter Three

The student as storyteller

'Students want to hear stories and sometimes want to tell them … there is no better way of developing fluency, than storying. Fluency for me means being able to make use of all the language you've got with the purpose of communicating meanings.'

Andrew Wright
Storyteller and author

Technique	Story	Page
From repeating to retelling	*Li and Gao*	94
From miming to retelling	*The Sleeve*	95
Mapping a story	*The Bridge*	96
Stepping through a story	*The Silver in the Fireplace*	98
Retelling a story in character	*How Spider Got a Narrow Waist*	100
Retelling a story in images	*Sand and Stone*	102
Creating a new ending	*The Talking Skull*	104
Performing a new ending	*The Snake and the King's Dreams*	106
From storytelling to storymaking	*The Seven Parrots*	108

From repeating to retelling

A telling technique

A simple and effective way to learn a story is through repetition – listening and telling the story again and again.

Li and Gao is such a well-known comic tale in China that it is referred to in everyday idiom, like *'Cry wolf'* is in English. I learnt it from a young Chinese woman called Jiamin.

To rehearse, concentrate on telling this tale clearly – and holding an audio-recording device steady at the same time.

Before telling

Ask for ideas about where would be a good place to hide a lot of money so nobody would find it. Tell the students they are going to learn to tell a very short Chinese tale, and encourage them to focus on your voice as you tell it.

While telling

Concentrate on telling the story to the students and recording yourself at the same time.

After telling

Invite the students, in pairs, to act out the whole story in mime. There will be no speaking, so they should act with a lot of physical expression: laughing to themselves, miming writing the note with great concentration (they are fools, after all!), digging with energy, etc.

Play the recording you made of yourself telling the story, and ask the students to make sure they understand everything.

The students listen again, this time focusing their attention on one or more of the following features, depending on what you know about their pronunciation:

Rhythm   Pausing   Word stress   Intonation
Linking words together   Vowel or consonant sounds

Now play the recording, pausing after each phrase and inviting the students to say the same phrase themselves.

They now tell the story aloud along with the recording – shadowing the voice pattern.

Ask pairs of students to sit facing each other – one will be the storyteller, the other the listener. It works best if the more confident storyteller goes first.
- Point out that, so far, they have been imitating *your* words, intonation and stress patterns.
- They are now ready to try telling the story in their own way, using their own words as much as they like.
- The listener supports the storyteller by making eye contact, and prompting if necessary. Then they exchange roles.

To follow on, make the audio recording of you telling the story available to the students online. Alternatively, they can follow the same procedure, listening to me at *www.worldstories.org.uk/stories/story/40-li-and-gao/english*. There is also a transcript of me telling the story – this might be useful to students who feel they cannot manage without written prompts.

You might also distribute the photocopiable worksheet 'Repeating and retelling' on page 33:
- The students can follow this procedure, which involves recording themselves, to learn the story.
- They can follow this procedure to repeat and retell *any* recorded story.

Note The procedure is adapted with permission from the 'Storytelling Guide for *Li and Gao*' in the Teachers Area of *www.worldstories.org.uk*.

Li and Gao

A Chinese tale

Li was a foolish neighbour. But one day, in the gambling house, Li won three hundred yuan.

'Ohhh, what shall I do with my yuan? Where shall I hide them? Where shall I store them? Ah, a good idea. I will store them in the ground.'

Li dug a hole and put the three hundred yuan into the hole. He covered the hole and then got a scrap of paper. He wrote on that scrap of paper and stuck it onto the ground.

It read: 'Three hundred yuan are not buried here.'

He had a jealous neighbour called Gao.

Gao knew that Li had won three hundred yuan, and was full of jealousy. He looked for where Li might have hidden them, and then he found that scrap of paper.

He dug up the three hundred yuan. He covered the hole. Then he found another scrap of paper and wrote on it and pressed it onto the ground.

On it were written the words:

'Gao did not steal three hundred yuan.'

From miming to retelling

A telling technique

The students retell a story their own way, using their own words, rather than imitating the storyteller.

The Sleeve is one of countless tales or jokes told in Western Asia, North Africa and the Balkans about the 'wise fool' Nasrudin. It is so well known that an everyday idiom in Turkish is *'Eat, oh my sleeve, eat!'* I was told *The Sleeve* by Yusef, who teaches Turkish in London.

To rehearse this story, mime reading the invitation, being sent away, putting on a long-sleeved kaftan – and letting the sleeve on your outstretched arm hang in the soup.

Before telling

Ask the students what they would wear to a dinner party at the house of an important person. Prepare them to listen to a short joke tale which they will be able to tell themselves afterwards.

While telling

Tell the story. Be clear and simple, bearing in mind that the students are going to have to remember and retell the story.

After telling

Invite the students, in pairs, to act out the whole story in mime. There will be no speaking, so they should act with a lot of physical expression – refusing entry, letting one sleeve dip in the soup, etc.

This tale is very short and simple so, having told the story *physically* – the students are now ready to retell the tale *verbally*.

Make sure they understand that they don't need to use exactly the same words *you* used, because learning to tell a story is a process of moving from imitating to 're-inventing'.

Ask the students to sit facing each other in pairs – one will be the storyteller and the other the listener.

- The storyteller can still use actions to support their telling of the story.
- The listener can support the storyteller by making a lot of eye contact, and prompting with mimes or verbally if necessary.

It works best if the more confident storyteller goes first. Then they can exchange roles.

To follow on, the students, in small groups, choose one of the discussion points from the list below:

- *What do clothes tell us about a person? Give examples.*
- *Talk about a time when you heard someone criticise someone else's way of dressing, either behind their back or directly to their face.*
- *Talk about a time when someone else criticised what you were wearing.*
- *What is the dress code in this classroom? What would be unacceptable?*

After a few minutes, a spokesperson from each group can briefly summarise the main points to the whole class for further discussion.

The Sleeve

A Turkish tale

A rich and important man sent Nasrudin an invitation to a dinner party.

When Nasrudin came to the party, he was still wearing his ordinary working clothes.

Nobody greeted him, not even the host.

He was not offered any food.

Instead, he was sent away.

Nasrudin went home and then returned, dressed in his finest kaftan with beautiful, wide, fur-lined sleeves.

He was warmly greeted by the rich and important host, and invited to sit at the table.

He reached for some meat, but his sleeve was hanging in the soup.

His host exclaimed, and pointed to the sleeve.

Nasrudin said:

'Eat, oh my sleeve, eat! You are the one who is invited to this party, not me!'

Mapping a story

A telling technique

One way for students to remember a story is to map a sequence of quickly-sketched images and use these as visual prompts as they retell the story. I learnt about storymapping in a workshop led by storyteller Chris Smith, who works with The Story Museum in Oxford, UK.

See: *www.storymuseum.org.uk/stories-at-school/ frameworksandtoolkits*

The Bridge is my retelling of a folk tale from Appalachia in the Eastern United States. It is a tale that often fills listeners with hope.

To rehearse, use a storymap as a prompt:

- Read the story just once and then take a blank sheet of A4 paper and sketch a sequence of about six images that will help you to retell the story.
- Link the images together with arrows to make a simple storymap.
- Spend no more than three minutes on this: the rougher your drawing is, the better.

Before telling

Say that you're going to tell a North American story about two friends, and that the students will be able to tell it themselves afterwards.

While telling

See the images you sketched in your mind's eye as you tell the story, but don't refer to your storymap. Pause a moment before you first say the word 'bridge'.

After telling

Hand out sheets of plain A4 paper and ask the students to spend three minutes drawing a bridge – as they think about the story. Then ask them to talk in pairs about the bridges they have drawn. Individual students can decide whether or not they *show* their drawings to their partners.

Explain that many people see pictures in their imagination as they listen to stories, and find out if any students didn't 'see pictures' as they listened to *The Bridge* (often there will be a couple who don't – because, like me, they experience the story powerfully through auditory and/or kinaesthetic channels).

Point out that one way of remembering the events of a story is to do a storymap – drawing a limited number of images as a sequence of very quick sketches linked by arrows.

- Tell the students that *you* drew six sketches when learning *The Bridge*, but only show them the back of your sheet of paper at this stage – so you don't influence what *they* draw.
- Tell them that they can learn to retell the story by each doing *their own* six-sketch storymap which no one else will see.

Tell the story again, suggesting that the students close their eyes and notice images while they listen.

Hand out blank sheets of A4 paper again.

- Before, they had *three* minutes to draw a bridge.
- Now, they need to do *six* images in *six* minutes.

Some students will probably finish with time to spare, while others will need to be encouraged to draw quickly.

Next, the students sit face-to-face in pairs and take turns to tell their version of *The Bridge*, referring with glances to their own storymap but without letting their partner see it.

- It's a good idea for the student feeling more confident in each pair to go first.
- The listener gives full attention to their storytelling partner and prompts them only if they request it.

After all the students have told the story for the first time, show them your own storymap, making it clear that there is no single correct way of mapping a story.

Ask the pairs to talk about how useful storymapping is for remembering the story. If they want to at this stage, they could show and talk about their own maps and compare them with yours.

The students tell *The Bridge* a second time to a different partner – this time, they should put away their storymaps and see the pictures they drew *in their mind's eye* as they retell the story.

To follow on, encourage the students to retell the story of *The Bridge* to people they know outside the class, and to be prepared to report back in the next class what those people said about the story itself and about the way they told it.

The Bridge

A North American story

There were once two shepherds, who had grown up together as best friends since they were young.

They lived near each other, grazing their flocks of sheep on the same hillside. They were close until, one fine spring morning, one of the shepherds said:

'Friend, you see that lamb following your flock? That lamb is one of mine. Give it back to me.'

'If it was yours, it would not be following its mother. The lamb is mine.'

'You are wrong. Look at its markings. It is clearly my lamb!'

The two became angry. They began to row. They shouted at each other. They nearly struck each other.

But they turned their backs and walked away from each other, back to their own homes.

From that moment, they stopped speaking. There were no greetings. They did not even look at each other. It was as if they had never been friends.

This went on for some time until, one evening as it grew dark, a stranger appeared, coming over the hill carrying a heavy bag on his back.

'Hey, stop! You look like a carpenter,' said one of the shepherds. 'I have a job for you. You see that house over there? I want you to build a strong fence for me between this house and that one; a fence so high that no sheep can jump over it, so high that no man can see over it. I will pay you well.'

The stranger said no word, but took his bag from his back.

The shepherd went to his bed, but he did not sleep well.

All night long, he was kept awake by the sounds of sawing and hammering. It was unusual that this carpenter was working through the night.

At dawn, the shepherd woke up to find the stranger standing in the doorway, his bag upon his back.

'Surely you haven't finished already?'

The stranger said no word, but walked away up the hillside. The shepherd stepped out through the door and into the morning sunshine.

There, between his house and the other shepherd's house, stood a strong and beautifully-made wooden bridge.

Stepping onto the bridge from the other side was his neighbour, the other shepherd, calling:
'Friend, what a fine idea to build a bridge between us. Our friendship is precious. Let us put our differences behind us.'

In the middle of the bridge, the two friends embraced, laughing with joy. Then they saw that the stranger was nearly at the top of the hill.

'Hey!' they called. 'Come back!'

The stranger turned and, for the first time, he spoke:

'I must go on. There are more bridges to build.'

Stepping through a story

A telling technique

The students 'step through' a story they have just been told, in pairs and section by section, remembering it kinaesthetically in preparation for retelling it.

The Silver in the Fireplace is an Afghan folk tale that I immediately wanted to retell when I found it under the title 'The Silver on the Hearth' in an anthology of folk tales from around the world titled *Ride with the Sun*, published in 1955 by the UN Women's Guild. That version was taken from *Some Current Pushtu Folk Stories* by F. H. Malyon, published in 1914.

To rehearse this tale, it is a good idea to mime actions such as warming yourself in front of the fire, clearing and digging up the brambles and reaching into the pot. This will make the story learning process simpler for the students.

Before telling

Let the students know that they are going to retell the story you are about to tell them.

While telling

Bear in mind that the students will be retelling the story, so keep the language you use clear and simple.

After telling

Invite a student who has a good grasp of the story to stand next to you.

- The student plays the role of the wife in the scene when she finds out about the pot of silver from her husband – played by you.
- You don't stick word-for-word to the text of the story you have told – just make sure the main ideas are the same.
- You may need to prompt the student – from within your role as husband – if some key information is missed.

The students now act out *the same scene* in pairs, all at the same time (but not as a chorus). The performances will, of course, all be different – in style, mood and physicality.

You might ask one pair of volunteers to show their scene to the class. The students watching give verbal feedback about one thing that impresses them in the pair's performance.

Next, 'step through the story' arm in arm with a confident student, remembering and retelling *the whole story* (see page 33 for more details). Take one step forward together at the end of each section.

All the students now step through the story in pairs – from the start and at their own pace. The fact that they have already acted out a scene from the middle of the story will make it easier for them to remember.

They then sit facing each other in the same pairs and take turns to tell the story. It makes sense if the more confident partner goes first.

To follow on, ask the students to retell the story a few times to different people outside the class.

- They can visit another group of students in another classroom, each finding a new partner – this time, they will be telling the story to someone who doesn't already know it.
- Alternatively, or additionally, this can be set as an oral homework task: the students tell the story to family members or friends.

By this stage, the students will be starting to innovate and 'make the story their own'.

The Silver in the Fireplace

An Afghan tale

There once lived a poor husband and wife in their little house.

Every day, the husband worked hard on their scrap of land, but they never had enough to eat.

Every night, he sat in front of the fire to keep warm until the wood had burned and the embers glowed, and every night he prayed:
'Let there be silver in the fireplace when I rise from my bed.'

Every morning, he woke at daybreak and prayed:
'Let there be silver in the fireplace when I rise from my bed.'

But when he looked, he found only ash.

One afternoon, as he was working the land, his clothes became caught on a bush of sharp brambles. After untangling himself from the brambles, he set about cutting the brambles back.

When he had finally cleared the brambles, he set about digging up the roots.

When he had finally dug up the roots, he found a large pot made of clay, so he set about opening the lid.

When he had finally opened the lid, he looked inside, and saw the pot was full of silver coins that shone in the sunlight.

He took a handful of silver coins and let them run through his fingers and laughed.

But then he remembered his prayer:
'Let there be silver in the fireplace when I rise from my bed. This silver is not in the fireplace and I have not just risen from my bed. This silver is not for me.'

Carefully he put the silver coins back in the pot and closed the lid. Then he buried the pot in the ground and returned home.

That night, he sat right in front of the fire to keep warm until the wood had burned and the embers glowed, and he prayed:
'Let there be silver in the fireplace when I rise from my bed, like the silver I found under the bramble bush today.'

His wife said, 'Silver under the bramble bush? What are you talking about, husband?'

'I found a pot of silver when I dug up the bramble bush, but it is not my silver because my silver will be in the fireplace.'
'Foolish husband! Go and fetch that silver now.'
'But it is not my silver because my silver will be in the fireplace.'

The wife went to their neighbour's house and knocked on his door.

'It's late. Is there a problem?' the neighbour asked.
'There is a pot of silver buried where the bramble bush was. Go and dig it up, and we'll share it.'

In the darkness, the neighbour went out, found the place where the bramble bush had been, and began to dig.

Soon he found the pot. Before he opened it he said:
'Why should I share the silver with my neighbours, when I am doing all the work? I'll take the silver for myself and leave and start a new life.'

The greedy neighbour carefully opened the pot and reached inside, but what he touched began to move, felt smooth and coiled around his hand. He quickly drew his arm out of the pot.

It was full of poisonous snakes.

He quickly closed the lid.
'My neighbours wish to kill me. I will give them what they deserve.'

He carried the large pot to his neighbours' house, and climbed up onto the roof. He emptied the poisonous snakes down their chimney.

In the morning, the husband woke at daybreak and prayed:
'Let there be silver in the fireplace when I rise from my bed.'

He rose from his bed, went over to the fireplace and looked.

'I have prayed for this, and so this is for me. Thank you. This morning, I have risen from my bed and my fireplace is full of silver.'

Retelling a story in character

A telling technique

The students retell a story they have just been told, from the perspective of a character.

How Spider Got a Narrow Waist is one of countless West African and West Indian tales about Anansi the Trickster, a demi-god who is both human and spider.

To rehearse this humorous and physical tale, pay attention to how you mime actions such as pulling and being squeezed, as well as the voice you give Anansi.

Before telling

Let the students know that Anansi the Man Spider is the trickster character in many West African and Caribbean folk tales. Sometimes he gets what he wants – but not always.

While telling

You could get the students to mime pulling on the threads.

After telling

Say: *Stand in pairs facing each other – A and B. It's a couple of days after the feast.*
A: You are one of the men who pulled on a thread.
B: You are one of the other villagers. You have just seen Anansi the Man Spider's new waist and you want to find out the whole story about how Anansi got such a narrow waist.
A: You want to tell the story, and will answer all of B's questions. Get ready …
3–2–1 Action!

After a few minutes, when the students have finished retelling the story from the villagers' perspective, say: *Choose 30 seconds from your storytelling and do it again. You know what you're going to say now, so focus on your voice and body. Get ready …*
3–2–1 Action!

Volunteer pairs show extracts of their storytelling in character to the whole class. Invite the listeners to comment on what they enjoyed about the different versions of the story. It may be that what happened to Anansi is interpreted in different ways:

- Some may believe that he deliberately lost weight, while others will see through his greed.
- Some may feel sorry for Anansi, some may laugh at him, while some may be envious of his narrow waist.

To follow on, talk about trickster characters the students know in folk tales in their own and other cultures:

- Foxes
- Coyotes
- Rabbits
- Monkeys
- Ravens
- Tortoises …

These are all tricksters from different cultural traditions.

The students can be asked to find a trickster tale and prepare to tell it to the class. They could refer to Kathleen Hempel's website: *Tricksters around the world*.

How Spider Got a Narrow Waist

A West African folk tale

Anansi – man spider, spider man – rested lazily between two hills; but he was so hungry.

He saw a man coming down one hill.

Anansi called out:
'Hey! Have you got something for me to eat?'

'Brother Anansi, I have nothing. But I'm going home to my village at the top of that hill opposite, and today we're going to have a great feast of spicy goat stew and corn mash. And I invite you.'

'Mmm, spicy goat stew, but that hill is so high.'

As Anansi looked up that hill, he saw another man coming down.

Anansi called out:
'Hey! Have you got something for me to eat?'

'Brother Anansi, I have nothing. But I'm going home to my village at the top of that hill opposite, and today we're going to have a great feast of fried chicken and plantain. And I invite you.'

'Mmm, fried chicken, but that hill is so high.'

The two men started going up the two hills.

'Wait!' called greedy Anansi. 'I want to come to both your feasts, so I can have spicy goat stew and fried chicken. But which feast will begin first?'

The two men could not say.

'I have an idea. Each of you take a strong thread as I weave it, and carry it up to your village. When your feast begins, pull on the thread and I will come. Then I can go to both feasts, first one and then the other.'

Anansi began to spin two strong threads at the same time, and each man took one and set off up the hills.

Anansi was spinning and spinning and spinning for a long time, and finally rested there, dreaming of the food, his mouth watering.

'Which will I have first, the spicy goat stew or the fried chicken, the fried chicken or the spicy goat stew?'

Which feast do you think began first? Can you guess?

Both feasts began at exactly the same moment.

The two men pulled on their threads at exactly the same moment.

Anansi was pulled in both directions at the same time.

The threads began to spin him around and around, and tangle around his middle.

The two strong men couldn't understand why Anansi wasn't coming, so they both pulled harder.

Anansi felt himself being lifted off the ground.

The strong threads were so tightly tangled around his middle that he couldn't cry out.

He could hardly breathe.

He was dangling there in mid-air.

The two men pulled harder still, and the knots around Anansi's middle became so tight that half his belly was pushed up above, and half his belly was pushed down below.

His waist became very, very narrow.

After a long time, all the spicy goat stew was finished at one feast, and all the fried chicken was finished at the other feast.

The two strong men wondered why Anansi hadn't come, so they came down from the two hills to find him.

As the threads loosened, Anansi slowly came back down to the ground. The knots were very tight but he skilfully managed to untangle them.

'Brother Anansi,' called the two men. 'Why didn't you come to the feast?'

Anansi smiled:
'I changed my mind. I wasn't really hungry. But look at me! Look at my beautiful narrow waist!'

Next time you find a spider in your bed, look closely – and you'll see it has a very narrow waist.

And now you know why.

Retelling a story in images

A telling technique

The students retell a story in groups, with each student visualising and describing one moment in sequence.

Sand and Stone is my retelling of a short wisdom tale I was told in 2012 by Faleh Alharbi, an Exeter University student from Saudi Arabia. I learned about retelling a story through describing moments in a brilliant workshop led by storyteller Hugh Lupton.

To rehearse this tale, aim to use minimal descriptive *language*. This will leave the students plenty of mental space to describe the *images* they create while listening to you.

Before telling

Say that you're going to tell a Middle Eastern tale about two friends, and that the students will be able to tell it themselves afterwards.

While telling

Remember to keep your telling clear and simple.

After telling

Tell the students that they are going to tell the story in groups – as a sequence of 'moments'. Get the class to agree on six moments which they think will tell the story well.

Write these up as notes so they are clearly visible to everyone. For example, the students might choose:

- Two friends crossing hot desert.
- Striking friend in anger.
- Writing in sand.
- Crossing desert in silence.
- Saving friend from quicksand.
- Carving in stone.

Ask the students to get into groups of six. Each student chooses a different moment from the displayed list.

Say: *Sit quietly and close your eyes if you wish. Imagine your answers to these questions:*

- *Can you feel the temperature at this moment in the story?*
- *Look at this moment in the story from a short distance away. What can you see around the two friends? … What light, what shadows, what colours? … Describe it in your imagination.*
- *Now step closer and let the picture become clearer … Look at the two friends. What do you see? … What clothes, what about their faces, their expressions? … Move around and look at them from different positions …*
- *Choose one of the friends. Reach out and put your hand on his shoulder … How is he feeling at this moment? What does he want?*
- *If this moment comes to life … What sound can you hear? Where is the sound coming from? How does the sound make you feel?*

Have these ideas in your head – as you open your eyes.

Ask the students to sit in pairs within their groups – each partner spends two minutes describing everything they imagined in their moment from the story.

Now ask them to edit their *two* minutes down to *one* minute, selecting the details they want to describe.

- In their group, they retell the story – in order, from moment 1 to moment 6 – as a series of images, listening closely to each other.
- After they have all finished telling the story, give them time to talk about the different ways different students imagined and described the story.

Ask them to individually tell the story to a partner from a different group, using any of the ideas they like from their group storytelling.

In the same pairs, the students can then talk about what they think of this short wisdom tale.

To follow on, encourage the students to retell *Sand and Stone* to people they know outside the class, and to be prepared to report back in the next class what those people said about the tale itself and about the way it was told.

Sand and Stone

An Arabian tale

Two friends were crossing the desert. The journey was long and they became thirsty and tired in the burning sun.

In his exhaustion, one traveller became angry and struck the other so that he fell to his knees in the sand. The man who had been struck wrote in the sand:

'Here, my friend struck me.'

The two travellers continued their difficult journey across the desert in silence.

After a long time, they could see a green oasis ahead of them.

The man who had been struck ran forward between the trees towards the cool water.

When he reached the edge, he began to sink down into the wet sand and could not climb back out.

Surely he would lose his life, sinking deeper down into the sand.

The other man ran forward, reached across the dangerous quicksand and pulled his friend to safety.

The man who had been saved took out his knife and carved words into a stone that stood nearby. It took a long time for him to write:

'Here, my friend saved me.'

'Why, when I hurt you, did you write it in the sand – but when I saved you, did you carve it in stone?'

'When you hurt me, I wrote it in sand so that soon the winds of forgiveness would blow the words away. When you saved me, I carved it in stone so that it will not be forgotten.'

Learn to write your hurts in sand, and to carve your blessings in stone.

Creating a new ending

A telling technique

The students can be invited to create and tell their own endings to an unfinished folk tale, first in pairs, and then as a whole class.

The Talking Skull is a gripping tale I have heard told in several variant forms from different cultures. This is my retelling of the version told by the Nupe people of Nigeria which I discovered in the introduction to Jane Yolen's *Favorite Folkales from Around the World* (Pantheon 1986). It contains a warning for storytellers who talk too much!

To rehearse, focus on the rhythm in the words. You could accompany yourself with a shaker to accentuate the rhythm (you can listen to me doing this on YouTube). Rhythmic speech can add magic and portent to a tale and stimulate student creativity.

Before telling

Say: *You're going to create your own ending to this story, so listen closely to the beginning.*

While telling

You could encourage the students to join in with the rhythm, perhaps by tapping on their thighs.

Stop when the hunter reaches the cave a second time, accompanied by the guards.

Say: *How do you imagine this story might end? Turn to a partner and listen to each other's endings closely. You might come up with two different endings, or perhaps you'll find an ending together.*

After the students have all listened to their partner's endings, ask for a volunteer to come to the front and tell their ending to the whole class.

- Ask the others to listen closely and notice similarities and differences to their own endings.
- Then ask for another volunteer – one who claims to have a very different ending – to tell theirs.

Once they have listened to three completely different endings, you could ask the students to tell their own ending again to new partner.

- They can tell their ending as before.
- Or they can include any ideas they like from the other students they have listened to.

Finally, ask the students to compare *their* endings with the *traditional* ending – as you tell it.

After telling

Say: *Don't talk for a minute … No talking … No talking at all. Think of people you know outside this class … Can you think of someone who talks too much? Remember one occasion when that person talked too much … What happened?*

After a minute of silent preparation, pair students who do remember an occasion together with others who don't – *their* task is to find out the details of what happened.

Ask the class: *What are the dangers of talking too much?* – and let them share their thoughts.

To follow on, invite the students to reflect on the different endings they made up and heard.

- They select their favourite ideas and, either individually or in pairs, write their own alternative endings to the story.
- They can put these up around the walls of the classroom as they finish.

The ones who finish writing first will have the chance to read more different endings, while those who need more time finish their endings.

The Talking Skull

A tale from West Africa

A young hunter left his village and climbed high, high, high into the mountains.

And there he found a cave.

And inside the cave there was a skull.

The skull greeted him.

'A talking skull? What brought you here?'

'Talking brought me here.'

The young hunter left the cave and down, down, down from the mountains he went, until he came to his village, and he went before the king.

'Up in the mountains there is a cave and inside the cave there is a skull, a talking skull.'

'Nonsense. A skull cannot talk.'

'It greeted me. It greeted you, Oh My King, and all of our people.'

'Guards! Go with this young hunter. See if what he says is true. If he lies, kill him.'

The young hunter and the guards left the village and high, high, high into the mountains they climbed, until they found the cave.

They went inside the cave.

And inside the cave was the skull.

The skull was silent.

'Greet me,' said the young hunter. 'Talk!'

The skull stayed silent.

So the guards drew their long knives, and they cut off the young hunter's head and they left the cave.

And after they had left the cave, the skull turned to the head and said, 'What brought you here?'

'Talking brought me here.'

Performing a new ending

A telling technique

The students create their own endings to a tale by improvising in role, before performing them.

The Snake and the King's Dreams is a folk tale from Georgia that I found in an anthology of folk tales from around the world titled *Ride with the Sun*, published in 1955 by the UN Women's Guild.

To rehearse, when you are looking for character voices for the King and the snake, it is a good idea if these are very distinct from each other and from your own 'narrator' voice. You could experiment with a booming voice for the King and a breathy voice for the snake – while also playing with pitch, volume, tempo, accent and attitude.

Before telling

Ask a student to do quick drawings of a fox, a sword and a sheep on the board. Around the pictures, you – or the students themselves – write anything the students associate with these.

While telling

Start the tale of the King's dreams, using your character voices for the King, Ivan and the snake.

After each dream, step into the role of the King and ask the students, as court advisors, to tell you what the dream means.

Listen to what they say and, still in the role of the King, respond to their ideas – before going on with the story.

Stop the story at the point when Ivan is returning with gold from the King's palace for the third time – and is about to meet the snake.

Ask all the students to work in pairs:
- They improvise their own endings to the story as a one-minute radio dialogue between Ivan and the snake. You encourage them to find voices for the two characters.
- Alternatively, the pairs can script and rehearse the dialogue.

A few pairs with different endings can perform their dialogues. The others listen, eyes closed.

Finally, you tell the *traditional* ending to the story.

After telling

The students discuss the snake's claim that all members of society conform to trends in behaviour, and that individuals have little control over their own actions.

To follow on, ask the students, in pairs, to think of occasions when they have experienced or witnessed non-conformist behaviour.
- The pairs script and perform a short 'radio sketch' based on one of these occasions, playing at least one role each.
- Encourage them to alter their voices.

After they listen to another pair's sketch, the students should identify the relationships between the characters, their feelings, the setting of the sketch and the nature of the non-conformist behaviour.

The Snake and the King's Dreams

A Georgian folk tale

The King ruled over a powerful land. One night, he had a dream.

He saw a fox hanging by its tail from the roof of the palace. In the morning, he called his advisors to him:

'In my dream, I saw a fox hanging by its tail from the roof of the palace. What does the dream mean?'

He was not satisfied with their answers, and could not forget the dream:
'Then everyone in the land must come before me. Whoever can explain the dream will be rewarded with gold coins.'

A poor peasant, called Ivan, set off from the other side of the mountains:
'I know nothing about dreams.'

He came to the high mountain pass and there, on the path, was a snake.

'Ivan, I will tell you the meaning of the dream if you promise to give me half of what the King gives you.
'I promise.'
'The fox hanging by its tail from the palace roof means that this is a land of lies and tricks. Remember: half for me.'

Ivan arrived at the King's palace and, when it was his turn, he stood before the King.

'Your majesty, the fox hanging by its tail from the palace roof means that this is a land of lies and tricks.'

The Snake and the King's Dreams

'This is surely the meaning of the dream. Ivan, take this bag of gold coins.'

Ivan set off for home and came towards the mountains.

'Why should I share this gold with the snake. If I take another route through the mountains, I can keep all the gold for myself.'

When Ivan reached his home, he lived off the gold.

Soon the King had another dream, and called his advisors to him:

'In my dream, I saw a sword hanging from the roof of the palace. What does the dream mean?'

He was not satisfied with their answers, and could not forget the dream, so of course he sent for Ivan.

'I know nothing about dreams. How can I answer the King? I'll have to find the snake.'

He came to the high mountain pass, and there was the snake.

'Ivan, I will tell you the meaning of the dream if you promise to give me half of what the King gives you.'
'I promise.'
'The sword hanging from the palace roof means that this is a land of hate and war. Remember: half for me.'

Ivan arrived at the King's palace, and was taken straight to the King.

'Your majesty, the sword hanging by its tail from the palace roof means that now this is a land of hate and war.'
'This is surely the meaning of the dream. Ivan, take this bag of gold coins.'

Ivan set off for home and came to the high mountain pass, where the snake was waiting for him.

'Ivan, give me my half of the gold coins.'
'The gold is mine. I will share it with no snake!'

Ivan drew his knife and went for the snake, but the snake quickly made for its hole. Ivan cut off just the end of the snake's tail.

When Ivan reached his home, he had more gold than he needed.

Soon the King had another dream, and called his advisors to him:

'In my dream, I saw a sheep hanging from the roof of the palace. What does the dream mean?'

He was not satisfied with their answers, and could not forget the dream, so once again he sent for Ivan.

'I know nothing about dreams. How can I answer the King? I'll have to find the snake.'

He came to the high mountain pass, but there on the path was no snake.

Ivan called for the snake and, finally, it appeared from its hole in the rocks.

'Ivan, I will tell you the meaning of the dream if you promise to give me half of what the King gives you.'
'I promise.'
'The sheep hanging from the palace roof means that this is a land of plenty and sharing. Remember: half for me.'

Ivan arrived at the King's palace, and was greeted personally by the King.

'Your majesty, the sheep hanging by its tail from the palace roof means that now this is a land of plenty and sharing.'
'This is surely the meaning of the dream. Ivan, take this bag of gold coins.'

Ivan set off for home and came to the high mountain pass, where the snake was waiting for him.

'Ivan, you have returned.'
'Yes, and this time I give you half of the gold coins.'

'I know, Ivan, I know ...
When you first came, it was a time of lies and tricks, and so it was with you. You cheated me. But what could you do, when you are one among many?
The second time you came, it was a time of hate and war, and so it was with you. You attacked me. But what could you do, when you are one among many?
Now you are here a third time, and it is a time of plenty and sharing. You want to share the gold coins with me, so blows the wind in the land. You are one among many. Ivan, I have no need of gold. Take your gold and go your way.'

And the snake made its way back to its hole
– and was gone.

From storytelling to storymaking

A telling technique

Students collaboratively create the complete second half of a longer story by responding to questions.

The Seven Parrots is a folk tale from Tamil Nadu in India. It was collected and published by Stuart Blackburn as 'A Parrot's Story' in his excellent book *Moral Fictions: Tamil Folktales from the Oral Tradition*, which I found here: www.storytellinginstitute.org/99.doc

To rehearse this tale, pay attention to the rich imagery and the repeated rhymes.

Before telling

Tell the students that they are going to create the *second* half of a folk tale from India together, so they need to listen closely to the *first* half.

While telling

Tell the first half of the story – up to the point where the ogre hooks his claws into the door.

Pause for a moment before starting to ask questions: this will enable the students to start to create the second half of the story collaboratively.

Ask mostly open questions:
• Questions that focus on moving the plot along:
    eg *What did she do next?*
• Questions that stimulate mental imagery:
    eg *What did she see/hear/smell/feel?*
Such questions inspire creativity and aid recall when students retell the story afterwards.

Make sure that every contribution is incorporated – by *restating* or, if necessary, *rephrasing* the students' contributions (see the example transcript on page 110).

You can facilitate the storymaking by reminding the students of unresolved narrative strands. For example:
What about the ogre's claws in the door?
What happened to them?
and guiding them towards the end. For example:
We're nearly at the end of the story …
so what did she do when the ogre was dead?

You could also play an extended and atmospheric piece of background music during the storytelling and storymaking. This can guide and inspire the students, and fill pauses with anticipation. A suitable piece of Indian music for this story might be Smt Kaushiki Desikan singing *Meera Bhajan* – you can find it on YouTube.

After telling

Once the story is at an end, ask pairs of students to immediately retell the second half of the story as they remember it. If necessary, *you* might retell the story first.
• Your restating and rephrasing of the students' contributions in the course of the storymaking provides a scaffold they can build on.
• However, because they have had ownership of the storymaking, they can add their own ideas as well.

Tell the traditional second half of the story and ask the students to notice similarities and differences between the versions. The students compare the two second halves in pairs, before sharing ideas as a whole class.

They are now ready to retell the whole story – the traditional ending, or their own ending, or a combination of the two.

To follow on, arrange for the students to rehearse and tell the story to people from other classes in the same institution.

The Seven Parrots
A story from India

There was a young goat-maiden, and she went with her brother and all the other children from the village to graze the goats near the forest. There, she saw a tree laden with heavy dark fruit, and she left the others and climbed into the tree's branches to pick and eat the delicious sweet fruit.

She didn't notice the ogre moving closer between the trees with his long, sharp, poisonous claws.

The other children ran away, with the goats following them, but the young maiden was stuck in the topmost branches of the fruit tree. The ogre below the tree called:

'Throw me down a fruit with your hands.'

The young maiden reached for a fruit with her hand and threw it down. The ogre caught the fruit, but he didn't catch the girl with his long, sharp, poisonous claws.

'Kick me down a fruit with your feet.'

The young maiden reached for a fruit with her foot and kicked it down. The ogre caught the fruit, but he didn't catch the girl with his long, sharp, poisonous claws.

The Seven Parrots

'Let me down a fruit with your hair.'

The young maiden reached for a fruit and tied it in her long black hair and let it down. The ogre caught the fruit, and he caught the girl. He pulled her down by her long black hair and carried her to the roof of his house.

One day, when the ogre was away, she looked up to see seven parrots with bright feathers flying down towards her. They lifted her up from the ogre's roof and carried her safely to their house.

The seven parrots took care of the young maiden until, one morning, they said:

'We must go away. Never open the door, or the ogre will catch you. You will know we are returning when you see a light shining in the well outside.'

The seven brightly-feathered parrots flew out through the door. The young maiden shut the door, went up onto the roof and watched them fly away.

She waited and waited until it was night.
She looked down the well, but there was no light.

The next morning she was hungry, but there was nothing to eat. Again, she went up onto the roof.

She waited and waited until it was night.
She looked down the well, but there was no light.

The next morning she was so hungry. She looked everywhere, but there was nothing to eat. Again, she went up onto the roof.

She waited and waited until it was night.
She looked down the well, but there was no light.

The young maiden opened the door and saw a house.

'Perhaps I can borrow a little food to cook.'

She knocked at the door. The door opened, and there was the ogre, reaching for her with his long, sharp, poisonous claws.

'This time, you won't get away!'

The young maiden turned and ran as fast as she could, but the ogre was just behind her, reaching for her with his long, sharp, poisonous claws in the darkness. She ran faster and into the parrots' house and shut the door. The ogre hooked two long, sharp, poisonous claws into the door: one high above and one down below.

She went up to the roof because it was night.
She looked down the well, and there was a light.

The parrots were flying back home! The young maiden ran and opened the door, but the two long, sharp, poisonous claws fell and pierced her flesh and killed her.

The seven parrots flew in through the door and squawked in sorrow:

'The beautiful maiden is dead.
The beautiful maiden is dead.'

The seven parrots made a beautiful box and put the young maiden's body inside. They flew, carrying the box to the sea. The box was carried by the waves to a distant shore.

There, a Raja and his minister found it.

The minister said, 'I shall have that box.'
The Raja laughed and said, 'Then I shall have what is inside the box.'

When the Raja opened the box, he found the lovely young maiden. He saw the two long, sharp, poisonous claws and pulled them out.

The maiden opened her eyes and took a breath of air.

The Raja took her to his palace and said:

'There were three brides for me to choose between, and now there are four. Whichever one of you can bring me the softest rice to eat will be my queen.'

He gave each bride a handful of rice, but the grains of rice still had their husks on. The other three brides began to pound the rice to get rid of the husks, but the young maiden sat and cried. At that moment she heard squawking, and she looked up to see the seven brightly-feathered parrots flying down towards her, squawking:

'The beautiful maiden lives.
The beautiful maiden lives.'

The seven parrots took the rice in their beaks and gently removed the husks.

The young maiden cooked the rice for the Raja.
The other three brides' rice was bruised, but the young maiden's rice was soft.

And so the goat-maiden became queen.

This is a transcript of the second half of *The Seven Parrots*
as it was being collaboratively created by a group of 30 young students.

Teacher: How did the girl feel inside the house …?

A student: **Worried, because the ogre was outside and she was still hungry.**

So what did she do …?

Another student: **She went to the roof and looked in the well.**

She went up to the roof because it was night, she looked down the well and there was a light … What did she see next …?

Fruit came from the sky.

What kind of fruit …?

Pears and mangoes.

What did the fruit taste like …?

It was divine fruit. It made her strong.

She ate the divine fruit which made her strong … and then …?

The parrots came back.

Where did the parrots come back from …?

Out of the well.

The parrots flew out of the well and their brightly-coloured feathers were shining. And she heard a sound. What did she hear …?

Their wings and voices: 'Aaark!'

She heard the parrots squawking and their wings flapping … What did she do …?

She opened the door.

She ran down from the roof and opened the door, and what happened …?

The ogre's claws flew out of the door and into her body.

And …?

She fell down dead.

She fell down dead. And where was the ogre …?

The ogre came and laughed and started eating her.

What happened when the ogre ate her …?

The poison from his claws went in his body and he became sick.

What happened next …?

The parrots flew in and pecked the ogre until he was dead.

And then …?

They put a magic feather in her mouth and she came back to life.

How did the parrots feel …?

They squawked for joy.

And how does the story finish …?

The girl went to the tree and picked a divine mango for the parrots. Then she went back to her village.

And is that the end …?

The feather inside her protected her for the rest of her life.

C

Storytelling With Our Students has so far offered you a grounding in the world of storytelling – by suggesting how you can put into practice the ideas and the 'telling techniques' outlined in Part A and Part B.

The first steps have been taken. So the time has come to explore further possibilities and opportunities for both you and your students.

Part C has been divided into three distinct sections: *In the classroom*; *Beyond the classroom*; and, finally, *Joining forces*, which suggests ways to continue your journey into the world of storytelling together with others, as an integral part of your ongoing personal and professional development.

In the classroom

Teacher storytelling

There are many more ways you can tell stories, still without leaving your classroom, that will add an extra dimension to your teaching.

Across lessons

Many folk tales are longer than the ones presented so far in *Storytelling with Our Students*.
- Longer tales can easily be broken down into episodes.
- Each one can be made to end on a 'cliffhanger'.

In this way, you can tell the story in parts over a number of lessons, and set creative tasks that the students can complete as homework activities in between.

Long tales

Telling a longer tale leaves plenty of scope for prediction and creating alternative versions. Here are just two examples:

The Silk Brocade is a beautiful Chinese story:
- *http://learningtogive.org/materials/folktales/SilkBrocade.asp*

Molly Whuppie is a thrilling Scottish tale:
- *www.sacred-texts.com/neu/eng/eft/eft23.htm*

Episodic tales

The bards of old would tell epics that continued night after night. Some of these long stories are 'tales within tales', such as *The Voyages of Sinbad* as they are told by Scheherazade in 'The Arabian Nights':

- *ww.sacred-texts.com/neu/lang1k1/tale15.htm*

When I tell even just one of Sinbad's seven voyages, I break it down into separate episodes.

Stories like *Sinbad* can be told as a story project over weeks. With each different episode, you can invite your students to do a different creative task like the ones set out in Part B.

Make sure the pattern has been established – the repeated pattern of voyage, of adventure and of return:

- There is then scope for the students to invent and tell parts of subsequent voyages themselves.
- There is scope for them to create their own 'Sinbad' voyages, individually or in groups.

Alternatively, retell a cycle of traditional stories such as *The High Deeds of Finn MacCool*, the great Irish hero, retold superbly by author Rosemary Sutcliff (Red Fox Classics). For example:

- You tell the first episode, which establishes Finn's birth and lineage.
- The students then work in pairs or small groups, each preparing to tell a different episode.

Across the curriculum

Storytelling fits well with language learning (both mother tongue and second language acquisition), drama, intercultural studies and personal development.

But storytelling has also a part to play in illuminating *other* subjects across the curriculum. For example:

- History, of all academic subjects, is based on stories. To what extent are legends such as *The Story of Sidwell* (see page 41) and folk tales like *The Witch of Tavistock* (page 59) based on actual historical events?
- Maths and Science can be brought to life for students when stories are woven into the teaching. In a Physics class, what better way to introduce Archimedes' Principle than by telling the Chinese story *How to Weigh an Elephant* (page 62)?
- Music and its role in society can be discussed after telling *Filling the House* (page 49) and music can also be improvised or composed to accompany or express sequences in a story.
- Law – the importance of the witness – is illustrated by stories like *The Fly* (page 87).
- Geology – the geological history of New Zealand – can be told in contrast with the creation myth *Maui and the Great Fish* (page 51).
- Philosophy, Ethics and Psychology are all best learned through stories such as *Dongguo and the Wolf* (page 77) and *The Small Bird's Wisdom* (page 73).
- Religion is at the heart of creation myths – such as *Ngaardi and Toonkoo* (page 45) – which can be compared with creation stories in dominant world faiths.
- Study Skills can be clearly illustrated and discussed through metaphor – see *The Teacher* on page 70.

Across languages

Mixed-language storytelling is an effective way of teaching a second language or target language to a class of learners who share the same mother tongue.

This works at all levels, but with beginner and elementary learners it is a good idea to choose a short folk tale the students already know well in their mother tongue. For example:

- Choose a universal tale, like *The Boy Who Cried Wolf*.
- See *Joha and his Donkey* on page 22.

Or you might like to tell a bilingual version of this Mayan story, *Rabbit and Jaguar*:

Rabbit and Jaguar
A mixed-language procedure

Preparation

Choose a simple story like *Rabbit and Jaguar* (see page 114) – ideally one which includes some repeated refrains – and prepare to tell it to your students without any written prompts. Find your own words: you don't need to stick closely to the text you have learned it from. Set aside a part of each of the next few lessons for the story.

In our example, English-mother-tongue (MT) students are learning Spanish as their target language (TL).

First lesson

Tell the story first entirely in MT except for a very small number of key nouns and verbs, or perhaps short phrases, which are repeated in the course of the story. The amount of new language will largely depend on the students' knowledge of TL.

- The first time you say these repeated TL words or phrases in the story, say them with extra emphasis while miming the meaning, and give a quick translation in MT. Use the same mime each time you repeat them.
- The second or third time, you may gesture to the students to repeat the words *after* you and then invite them to repeat the words *with* you. You may even get to the point where you gesture to the students to say the words *instead of* you.

After telling the story, say (and possibly write up) the TL words or phrases you used, and ask for MT translations.

Invite the students in pairs to ask each other (in MT or TL, depending on their level) what they like about the story.

Second lesson

A few days later, tell the same story again and, this time, use further TL vocabulary in addition to putting the vocabulary that you used in the first telling into short TL phrases. Bear in mind that the students are likely to remember and understand the TL used in the context of a well-told story. After telling the story, find out how much the students think they understand. This time, ask them to translate vocabulary from MT to TL.

Third lesson

The next time you tell the story, tell it mostly in TL. You can still translate (directly or paraphrasing) some phrases into MT, according to what your students need. Encourage the students to participate chorally in the storytelling, wherever there are repeated phrases or they remember key words in TL.

Next lessons

Continue this process until you can finally tell the whole story in TL, knowing the students understand more and more each time. You will see their confidence increase when they can learn TL through MT, using this step-by-step approach.

Option

You could display or hand out a written version of the story in TL which is close to the way you tell it.

- If you are introducing your students to a new alphabet or script for the first time, you might point to the words as you retell it.
- If they are already familiar with the TL script, they can do this independently.

Extension

The students can retell this story themselves, in the same way you told it to them, without the support of the text, using a combination of MT and TL. The more people they tell the story to, both inside and outside the classroom, the more confidence they will have in their own TL skills.

I would like to acknowledge Mario Rinvolucri and Sheelagh Deller, who wrote about this approach in their invaluable resource book *Using the Mother Tongue* (Delta Publishing 2003).

Rabbit and Jaguar
The beginning of the story

First telling

There lived, once, an old man and an old woman. And all they had in the world was one **conejo** (a rabbit) and one **jaguar** (a jaguar).

They kept **Conejo** in a **jaula** (cage).

One day, **Jaguar** came to the **jaula**: 'Oh, Rabbit ... ! **Conejo** ... ! The old man and the old woman are preparing a pan of hot water. They are going to boil you. They are going to eat you. They are going to give some to me.'

'Oh no,' said **Conejo**. 'No indeed. They are going to make hot chocolate. And if you come in the **jaula** with me, they will bring some for you, **Jaguar**.'

Jaguar opened the door of the **jaula** and slinked inside. With a hop and a skip, **Conejo** was out of the **jaula** and away through the door of the house.

Jaguar waited there, and waited there, and waited there some more … **Jaguar esperaba y esperaba y luego esperó unos minutos más ...**

'I've been tricked! There is no hot chocolate!'

Jaguar leapt out of the **jaula** and out through the door, and through the forest he went, looking for where **Conejo** had gone …

Second telling

Había una vez an old man and an old woman. And all they had in the world **eran un conejo y un jaguar**. They kept **el conejo en una jaula**.

One day, **Jaguar** came to **la jaula**: 'Oh, Rabbit ... ! **Conejo** ... ! The old man and the old woman **están preparando** a pan of **agua caliente**. They are going to **cocerte**. They are going to **comerte**. They are going to **compartirte conmigo**.'

'Oh no,' **dijo Conejo**. 'No indeed. **Van a preparar chocolate caliente**. And if you come in **la jaula conmigo**, they will bring some for you, **Jaguar**.'

Jaguar opened **la puerta de la jaula y entró**. With a hop and a skip, **Conejo** was out of **la jaula** and away **por la puerta de la casa**.

Jaguar **esperaba y esperaba y luego esperó unos minutos más ...**

'I've been tricked! There is no **chocolate caliente**!'

Jaguar leapt out **de la jaula** and out **por la puerta**, and through **el bosque** he went, looking for where **Conejo** had gone …

Third telling

Había una vez una pareja de ancianos: an old man and an old woman. **Las únicas cosas que tenían en el mundo entero eran un conejo y un jaguar.** They kept **el conejo en una jaula. Un día, Jaguar** came to **la jaula y dijo:**

¡Oh Conejo, Conejo! Están preparando una cazuela llena de agua caliente. They are going to **ponerte dentro para cocerte y** they are going to **compartirte conmigo.**

'Oh no,' **dijo Conejo, 'No es cierto. Van a preparar chocolate caliente, y si entras en la jaula conmigo, Jaguar, te darán una taza** – they'll give some to you.

Jaguar abrió la puerta de la jaula y entró. De un salto – with a hop and a skip – **Conejo se escapó de la jaula y salió por la puerta de la casa.**

Jaguar esperaba y esperaba y luego esperó unos minutos más ...

¡Me ha engañado! I've been tricked! – **¡No hay chocolate caliente!**

Jaguar salió de la jaula, corrió por la puerta y fue al bosque a buscar a Conejo ...

You can find the complete English and Spanish versions of this wonderful story in the Spanish section of the World Stories website:

- *http://www.worldstories.org.uk/stories/story/37-the-rabbit-and-the-jaguar/english*
- *http://www.worldstories.org.uk/stories/story/37-the-rabbit-and-the-jaguar/spanish*

My thanks to World Stories for welcoming the inclusion of this story and these ideas in *Storytelling With Our Students*.

This procedure is reproduced from the Advice Article – 'Mixed Language Storytelling' – in the Teachers Area of *www.worldstories.org.uk*.

Student storytelling

Your students can also select stories themselves to bring into class, or they can be asked to create brand new ones of their own to tell.

Bringing their own stories

Once the students have become accustomed to interacting with, and retelling, tales they are told, they are ready to find, rehearse and tell tales of their own choice in class. It is a good idea to set a time limit of four or five minutes at first.

They might choose favourite short folk tales they have been told outside the class, or they can search in collections in books or online for stories they *would like* to tell and which they feel they *can* tell. You might need to direct them to suitable sources – the ones from page 122 are highly recommended.

The students can use techniques they have tried before, such as storymapping (see page 33) and stepping through a story (page 33) to learn and rehearse their stories.
- Encourage them to find their own words and to audio- and video-record themselves, in order to evaluate and improve their own performances while they rehearse.
- Encourage them to use every opportunity to tell the story to others and get feedback, before they tell it in class.

The students should first tell their stories in pairs to warm up.
- Ask them to comment on what they enjoy about their partner's storytelling.
- Then ask them to split from their partner and get into groups of four, to listen to each other's storytelling.

Over the following weeks, you could start each lesson with one student telling their story to the whole class. The storytelling student can then set the listeners a brief response task – such as *Tell your partner one thing that interested you about the story*.

In fact, any of the activities in this book can be used with stories told by students. For example, *Interacting through different cultures* on page 66 offers opportunities to compare very short stories that are at once both different and similar.

When the students are becoming confident classroom storytellers, they can organise their own 'storytelling festival' and invite other students, staff and families.

Creating their own stories

Students who are used to listening and responding to stories imaginatively are well-placed to create stories from scratch – as long as a framework is provided. Collaborative and improvised storytelling activities – like the one below – reveal how incredibly creative student storytellers can be.

The Find
A collaborative storymaking procedure

Preparation

You will need to prepare an attractive box containing small shiny objects (including a crystal, a lump of fake gold, a coin, a ring, a star and a shell) and atmospheric instrumental music. For example, if you'd like to set the story in China, you could play traditional Chinese instrumental music – such as at *www.youtube.com/watch?v=7IsLCqMml8I*. Of course, the music you select is going to affect the kind of story that emerges.

Procedure

Invite the students to sit in a circle, then put on the background music and you all listen together for 30 seconds.

Speaking in the first person, begin: *I was lost and alone, and I was walking … What could I see around me?*

- Once several students have raised a hand to show that they have an answer, invite one of them to say their answer, and accept it.
- Continue establishing the story by asking open questions – such as: *What time of day was it?* and *How did I feel?* – and incorporating the answers.

Your role is to provide the framework, while allowing the students creative freedom. After about a minute, say: *Suddenly I noticed something small and shining on the ground in front of me … a small shining object … What was it?*

Wait for a student's answer, take out the corresponding shiny object from the box you have prepared, and hold it out on the palm of your hand for the students to admire. Ask: *How did I feel when I saw it? … What did I do? … What magical thing happened?*

Continue the story, incorporating student input and asking further open and sensory questions in response to their contributions, such as: *How did I feel? What did I hear? Where was the voice coming from? Can you describe the old man?*

- Invite input from the whole class – to ensure that they will *all* feel part of the creative process.
- Accept and respond to every contribution – this is fundamental to improvised storymaking.

The storyline can go in any direction. However:

- Bear in mind that a good story involves the main protagonist facing a problem, and that the problem needs resolving.
- Guide the students towards the conclusion of the story by asking: *We are nearly at the end of the story – what did I need to do?*

When they have finished, the students retell the story they have created in pairs. They tell it in the third person, as a folk tale, beginning: *Once there was a young man/woman who was lost and alone, …*

- Remember that, because the story is *theirs*, the students are free to alter the story and make it their own as they retell it.
- Note that, when you incorporate students' answers into the story, you will naturally reformulate and extend the language they use. This provides scaffolding, for when it comes to their retelling the story.

Finally, ask pairs of students to act out a scene from the story they have created – a suitable scene would be one where the protagonist interacts with another character.

Option

Once the story is well-established and it is clear that the shining object is integral to the whole narrative, hold it out solemnly.

- A volunteer student can take it and continue in the role of 'first person storyteller'. Make sure they solicit and incorporate other students' ideas.
- Another volunteer can take on the storytelling role, and you might prompt the class to reincorporate some characters and events from earlier in the story, in order to guide this storyteller to the ending.

Slowly turn down the volume of the music to silence. See the example on YouTube – 'David Heathfield: Storymaking with Chinese Learners of English':

- *www.youtube.com/watch?v=L0_7I5iFYrg*

Extension

The students, in groups of three or four, can create their own stories in the same way.

- Put on the music again, so that each group can create their tale.
- Once they have finished, students from different groups can form pairs.
- They retell and compare their stories.

There is a great sense of achievement resulting from creative storytelling of this kind.

This procedure is adapted from an activity published in *Speaking Spontaneously* (English Teaching Professional 38, 2005).

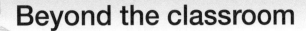

Beyond the classroom

Teacher storytelling

Storytelling in class brings story landscapes alive in the listeners' imaginations, but of course storytelling is also effective in a wide variety of locations beyond the classroom – giving a sense of place and connecting people with the environment. Because stories generally require no more physical resources than the teacher and the students, they can happen anywhere – as long as noise and other distractions do not prevent listening.

Outdoors

This sense of 'belonging' is particularly in evidence in world cultures where spirituality and landscape are inseparable – such as in Native American and Australian Aboriginal societies – but this interconnectedness is there in traditional stories worldwide, and is part of everyone's heritage.

Many traditional folk tales are set in the natural world and when you tell them in a natural environment, another dimension is added to the experience. Students often feel a connection between the imagined world of the story and the sensory experience of being in a parallel physical environment.

The setting and the story The day before I wrote this, the early summer sun was shining and I told the story of *Juan and the Magic Tree* (page 56) to a group of 30 young students under a tree in their school grounds.

A teacher commented afterwards that, during and after the storytelling, the landscape seemed more vibrant.
- The students were conscious of the dark and gentle shade given by the tree, the coolness of the growing grass they were sitting on, the movement of the air around them and the sound of the leaves rustling in the breeze.
- Some of them imagined the trunk of that very tree splitting open and the goat stepping out – just as in the story.

Of course, the setting also affects the *way* you tell a story.
- Details of the surroundings at the moment of the storytelling might find their way into the language you use, so that they are intertwined with the world of the story.
- The stick from the story of Juan might become a stick you pick up from under the tree as you tell the tale.

That environment at that moment will, from then on, be the setting of that story in the students' imaginations – and the story will be remembered each time they sit under that tree.

The story and the setting It even makes sense to *change* elements of a story to fit in with the environment and the season. A storymaking activity like *The Find* (page 115 above) is particularly suited to settings outside the classroom, where features and items within the students' immediate environment are woven into the story as it is created.
- If you tell *The Small Bird's Wisdom* (page 73) in a garden in spring, describe the scent of the flowers and refer to a bird you can actually see there.
- If there is snow on the ground outside on a particularly cold winter's day, you might decide to tell *Aldar Kose Tricks the Bai* (page 75) when the students have just come in out of the cold.
- And you can encourage them to create their own 'snow child' outside – just after listening to *The Snowgirl* (page 83).

Indoors

This, of course, does not apply exclusively to stories set outdoors.

- You might be visiting an old house with your students, and can adapt the way you tell *Filling the House* (page 49) so that the story is taking place in that very house.
- You might tell *The Sleeve* (page 95) while sitting round a table and sharing a celebratory meal with your students.

The possibilities of connecting a story to the place and time it is being told in are endless.

Online

Storytelling is becoming increasingly popular online, especially now that face-to-face communication technology is becoming more widely used.
- It can happen across unlimited distances, both on a one-to-one basis and with very large communities of listeners.
- I recently did a large online cross-cultural storytelling webinar/workshop with the British Council in Turkey. I told a story with several hundred teachers listening live, and hundreds more listening afterwards.

Many of the stories I have told with students, including all of the stories in this book, are available on YouTube.
- You can watch me telling them with students in a variety of contexts.
- And if *you* decide to share video-recordings of *yourself* and *your* students telling stories online, please let me know – *david@davidheathfield.co.uk*.

Student storytelling

As your students develop their *classroom* storytelling skills, it makes sense for them to share the stories they are telling with as many others as possible *beyond* their classroom. As well as storytelling in a variety of *locations*, as mentioned above, it is worth considering who their *listeners* might be.

Different classes, different stories

Your students can prepare to tell stories to students from another class, typically from a class at a parallel or earlier stage of language development.
- This can be during class time, so that you can support your students through the process and pair them with suitable partners.
- If different students have prepared different stories, then they can each tell their story more than once. Their second and third tellings will nearly always be more satisfying than the first.

Family, friends and guests

Also, the students can tell their stories to people they know outside the classroom.

Connecting storytelling in class with storytelling in the family is of great benefit.
- Ask the students to tell their story two or three different times, to two or three different people, *outside class*.
- Invite your students' friends or family members *into the class* to be told – or even to tell – stories.

Because of the reciprocal nature of exchanging stories, students tend to bring stories back and forth between home and classroom – and enrich the lives of their fellow students and family members by doing so.

The next stage can be for the students to tell stories to small groups of invited listeners.
- For this, consider spreading the storytelling out into different physical spaces.
- It is likely to be distracting if several stories are being told in the same place simultaneously.

Multi-media projects

In some schools, several classes do arts projects on a common theme at the same time, which culminate in a shared event including performances and displays. Student storytelling sits well alongside visual artwork and music, and gives a powerful focus to events like these.

- One class of mine – who were learning about 'fair trade' food – told world folk tales on the theme of food in front of large-scale student paintings of crops, harvests and transport.
- The storytelling was interspersed with performances of percussive music and song, inspired by traditional music from different regions of the world.

Festivals and community events

School students can participate in festivals in the local community, or organise their own community storytelling 'festival'.

- An intimate storytelling space can be created in a classroom or hall – by reorganising the furniture and decorating it to reflect the kind of stories being told.
- A tent in a quiet outdoor area is particularly suitable for storytelling, as it provides an outdoor, close-to-nature festival atmosphere and, at the same time, encloses the listeners in the world of the story.

For the last few years I have organised the World Storytelling Tent at the annual Exeter Respect Festival, a two-day community event celebrating cultural diversity in the city where I live. This year, we collaborated with the Exeter Royal Academy for Deaf Education.

- The storytelling was interpreted into British Sign Language, and we also had BSL storytelling being interpreted into English.
- This brought together students from the deaf and the hearing communities in Exeter in a shared cultural experience.

It is wonderful to host an event where professional storytellers and young people from the local schools have the opportunity to perform in the same storytelling space.

Joining forces

You can use *Storytelling With Our Students* to develop your own storytelling skills – both individually and independently. But you might also be in a position to set aside time with *other* teachers to learn and develop as storytellers *together*. This can lead to the evolution of a storytelling community.

Peer workshops

One way to learn together is in workshops of any size, even in pairs. In my own case, I share a teaching job with my wife Tammy, and we often try out storytelling ideas with each other before we do them with our students.

- You could agree together in advance what you would like to learn from the next workshop, and focus on one or more techniques.
- Alternatively, each individual could come to the workshop with a *different* focus.

Below is the outline of a workshop for teachers who want to focus on the kind of core techniques described in this book, in order to develop their own classroom storytelling skills.

- The teachers come to the workshop with a short folk tale, or part of a folk tale, they are preparing to tell with their students.
- They split into groups of three, and each teacher takes a turn.
- The teacher briefly describes the profile of the students, and how the storytelling might benefit their learning. It works well if the teacher identifies a particular aspect of their storytelling they are uncertain about, and asks their two peers to pay attention to that. For example: 'how to get students to participate verbally in the storytelling'.
- The two peers listen to the teacher telling the story, while paying attention to the aspect in question.
- After the storytelling, the two peers comment positively and briefly on what they enjoyed

most about the storytelling. It is important to ensure that colleagues support each other by giving constructive, formative feedback – and not being overcritical.

- The storytelling teacher then focuses on the agreed aspect and leads the feedback, using questions beginning *What if I …?* For example:
  What if I became the king and asked the students what to do?
  What if I allow more time for the students to answer the question before continuing?
- The peer teachers respond, and encourage the storytelling teacher to try out different ideas *there and then*. This opens up possibilities that may never otherwise have been considered.

Once all the teachers in all the groups of three have had their turn, they tell the same story again in different groups of three, and try out the new ideas they have explored. This time, the listening teachers can play the role of students who are listening to their favourite storytelling teacher.

These *What if …?* questions empower storytelling teachers:
- They are leading the exploration of their own storytelling themselves.
- They are making their own choices about which ideas to accept and reject.
- They are more prepared for trying out new storytelling techniques with their students.

And, of course, the peer *listening* teachers can learn just as much in *their* role.

Other ways to share storytelling skills are for teachers to open classroom doors:
- They invite each other in, or put classes together.
- They do team-storytelling with the whole of, or sections of, the school community.

This peer-sharing process can also be used when trying out different ways *into* and *out of* a story (see Chapter Two in Part B of *Storytelling With Our Students*) – and, in fact, in most other areas of teaching practice.

Training workshops

You might invite an established storyteller who also offers teacher training workshops to come into your school. The teachers can observe their students' responses to what the storyteller does.

They can then do a workshop, or series of workshops, in which they try out techniques and build up their skills.
- One of the most satisfying aspects of my own work is to do workshops of this kind with developing classroom storytellers in the UK and around the world.
- Sometimes I have the pleasure of sharing skills with a group of teachers over a period of months, during which time they make huge strides in terms of confidence and ability.

Teachers comment that this has a transformative effect on their students' learning, too.
- For some teachers, it is easier to learn by doing workshops, and through reflective practice with others, than by working through a book like this.
- For others, the ideal may be a combination of the two.

What you do – the steps you take – will depend on you and your personal and professional situation.

Courses

There are excellent storytelling courses for teachers.

There are storytelling workshops and courses, mostly UK-based – and not just for teachers – listed on the 'Events' pages of the Society for Storytelling website:
- *http://www.sfs.org.uk/events*

I am an associate teacher trainer with Horizon Language Training in Devon, UK:
- *www.horizonlanguagetraining.co.uk*

Comments

Below are some adapted and abbreviated comments from participants in the Horizon Storytelling course, which give an interesting perspective on the wider implications of storytelling for the teacher-storyteller, the language learner and the language classroom.

'A completely new world. It has changed my outlook on teaching.'
Odile Verdier (France)

'As a secondary school teacher, it made me realise how much fun storytelling can be in the classroom for both students and teacher.'
Janet Romunde (Holland)

'I realised the importance of storytelling not only in primary schools but also in high school, which is where I teach. Storytelling helps me in teaching literature.'
Maria Concetta (Italy)

'It made me go back to when I was a child and used to enjoy stories. Stories help you to successfully teach grammar and vocabulary. There is no need for sophisticated devices: some words, sentences or drawings are enough, and any class of English becomes fun. Students love stories … they become active, and their creativity is amazing. They completely change their attitude … talking, sharing ideas, giving opinions. No more bored students; happy teacher; successful classes.'
Liliana Gherghinescu (Romania)

'I was not an innate storyteller. I expected to gain some techniques to be more self-confident despite my 'handicap'. The most important thing I learned is that the teacher or the students do not have to be highly-talented storytellers to enjoy and benefit from storytelling. There are many techniques and activities from which you can choose to suit your talents or your personality.'
Susana Pascual Safont (Belgium)

'Stories and the connected activities exercise an irresistible power – ideas and emotions come out and mix up with other people's. As adults, we sometimes undervalue the richness of stories. I think it's important to use of this power to give my students the chance to know stories from all over the world: it's also a natural way to connect children from different countries and cultures.'
Monica Bertasi (Italy)

'I have discovered a side of me I didn't know existed. I have started telling stories in class, and my students are not even aware they are learning English, they just enjoy listening. My largest class consists of 32 students and, when I tell a story, you can hear a pin drop. And we're talking about 15 year olds. That's quite an achievement.'
Beike En Henri (The Netherlands)

'It changed my teaching philosophy. I have since worked a lot with illiterate adult immigrants and made huge progress, after having realised that nearly everything can be taught in the form of a story. So any everyday situation (actions, vocabulary, emotions, humour, misunderstandings) can be served as a whole package, and the learners are capable of digesting relatively big chunks of language. As I haven't a common language with my learners, I do a lot of acting and mime, which they appreciate very much.'
Irma Partanen (Finland)

'They demonstrated different stories – anecdotes, picture stories, dramatisation, legends, etc – and even how they could be used in teaching the mother tongue. The teachers also used a multi-sensory approach in language teaching: this makes easy the perception of the school material by students of different ages, and also by students with disabilities.'
Yordanka Peshevska (Bulgaria)

'I have used your ideas hundreds of times … to the point that I have become a teacher trainer in the local teacher training database (Rhône-Alpes). I have been able to get my students to participate more in their learning process, to have more fun in class and to dare to speak more in front of the group in varied contexts.'
Elise Peizerat (France)

Sources

Please note that I give the URLs for the online sources – but you can sometimes find them more comfortably by simply searching by name.

Storytelling With Our Students

The stories

If you search for David Heathfield on YouTube, you will find me telling all the tales in this book to teenage and adult learners of English, and there are many other live stories besides.

I put these videos on YouTube to share my storytelling ideas – but I urge you to tell stories *yourself* with your students, rather than to show them recordings of me on a screen – with debatable production quality.

The activities

You can watch students doing several of the activities as they appear, in the form of storytelling procedures, in *Storytelling With Our Students*.
- Look on YouTube for David Heathfield and the activity title.
- Look on page 36 of this book for a list of videos available at the time of writing.

The plan is to video more of the activities with my students, as time goes by – in which case, there should be more examples for you to watch in the future.

Sources and resources

There are many different ways to tell stories, and to lead into them and lead out of them – and to learn from them. If you take the time to look into some of the resources listed below, you will be well rewarded.

Storytelling skills development

The Storyteller's Way by Ashley Ramsden and Sue Hollingsworth, who teach at the International School of Storytelling, is an excellent resource for groups supporting each other as they realise their potential as storytellers. (Hawthorn Press 2013)

Personal and group development

Dr Alida Gersie demonstrates how creation myths from indigenous cultures can be sources of deep personal learning.
- *Earthtales* – no longer in print, but do your best to get hold of a used copy if one becomes available online. (Green Print 1992)
- *Storymaking in Bereavement* (Jessica Kingsley Publishers 1992)
- *Storymaking in Education and Therapy* with Nancy King (Jessica Kingsley Publishers 1990)
- *Reflections on Therapeutic Storymaking* (Jessica Kingsley Publishers 1997)

The myths are integral to activities which give group members insight into themselves and each other, and make them able to deal with change.

Teacher development

- Mario Rinvolucri shares brilliant storytelling ideas on the British Council Teaching English website:
  www.teachingenglish.org.uk/think/articles/story-telling-language-teachers-oldest-technique
- *Once Upon a Time*, the groundbreaking teachers resource book by Mario Rinvolucri and John Morgan, introduces teachers of English to a broad range of stories and classroom activities for teenage and adult students. (CUP 1983)
- *Imagine That!* – another of Mario Rinvolucri's books, which is co-authored by Jane Arnold and Herbert Puchta – has a strong storytelling focus. (Helbling Languages 2007)
- *Storytelling with Children* (OUP 2009 2nd edition) and *Creating Stories with Children* (OUP 2007) by Andrew Wright are must-haves for teachers of young learners.
- *Storytelling in ELT* is a selection of folk tales, each one selected by a different teacher and with its own English teaching lesson plan devised by that teacher. (IATEFL 2003)

Various videos – various viewpoints

There are also videos of me telling stories – not only with a variety of listeners, but also with a variety of accompaniments and in a variety of locations:

Listeners and learners

- Pre-school children – *Brer Fox and the Bunnies*
  www.youtube.com/watch?v=UgLC-ghIZP4
- Schoolchildren – *Mother Holle*
  www.youtube.com/watch?v=IZvZrrebE5c
- Teenagers – *The Washergirl and the Count*
  www.youtube.com/watch?v=czpkjqUKHPg
- Adults – *The Tale of Ivan*
  www.youtube.com/watch?v=fACfrdhM_is
- Older people – *The Fairy Ointment*
  www.youtube.com/watch?v=Udh0uxM5SIA
- Young learners of English – *The Island of the Sun*
  www.youtube.com/watch?v=RihKTLCuYic
- Families – *The Mitten*
  www.youtube.com/watch?v=fXWVoBHulbg
- People with learning difficulties – *The Girl who was Sold with the Pears*
  www.youtube.com/watch?v=5m9W3tbE1lw

Sounds and music

- Sound effects – *The Magic Pipe*
  www.youtube.com/watch?v=EaTOq6yptlM
- Music – *Anansi and the Stories*
  www.youtube.com/watch?v=DmlKXeDKVAw
- Percussion – *The Singing Drum*
  www.youtube.com/watch?v=3mQYI1frSqg
- Song – *The Heathfield Hare*
  www.youtube.com/watch?v=Ka7x54uNixg
- With a musician – *The Tale of Ahmed*
  www.youtube.com/watch?v=xd_gwOiA4oY
- With a dancer – *The Royal Flea*
  www.youtube.com/watch?v=V-0ceTuY2Gs

Spaces and places

- At intercultural events – *The Shepherd and the Snake*
  www.youtube.com/watch?v=QJct87JjA_M
- At festivals – *The Golden Goose*
  www.youtube.com/watch?v=J7goGE8M2Gg
- In the local community – *The Future*
  www.youtube.com/watch?v=v3B0pjNcKa4
- Outdoors in summer – *How Anansi Got a Narrow Waist*
  www.youtube.com/watch?v=kiI30uuuLdI
- Outdoors in winter – *The Great White Beast of the Dovrefell*
  www.youtube.com/watch?v=zZfTA0JnHOI

Not only, but also ...

- Multisensory features – *The Three Feathers*
  www.youtube.com/watch?v=eIXYEJb3o5E
- Based on history – *Bill Brewer's account of the Exeter Blitz, 4 May 1942*
  www.youtube.com/watch?v=tnMEo3DW4s4
- In Spanish – *Orejas Largas*
  www.youtube.com/watch?v=Aj2sSHpRY5c

Collective storytelling projects

Here are two useful online materials resulting from storytelling projects in which I have had the privilege of collaborating with other storytellers:

- World Stories is a resource with which I am involved and which is for students and teachers. Stories are told and written both in English and the languages they come from. There are audio recordings of me telling fourteen stories from around the world, as well as the transcriptions. When you log in (for free) to the Teachers Area, you can find Storytelling Guides written for teachers, which go with those fourteen stories: *www.worldstories.org.uk*
- Project Grimm is one of the most fascinating projects I have had the pleasure of taking part in. Videos of storytellers telling versions of all 200 Brothers Grimm fairy tales in different European languages are here to be enjoyed: *http://projectgrimm.blogspot.co.uk*

Individual storytellers

There are countless other storytellers on YouTube – here is a diverse selection of some favourites of mine:

- Baba the Storyteller often rhythmically accompanies his wonderful storytelling, playing the African 'kora' – you can watch him telling another version of *The Bridge* (page 97) with third graders: *www.youtube.com/watch?v=N5R21dk69BQ*
- Traditional Tuvan storyteller Shoydak-Ool tells *Boktu Kirish*, an outrageous and magical Tuvan epic, outside a yurt on the plains of Southern Siberia – a timeless experience – with English subtitles: *www.youtube.com/watch?v=Ha1dFpiVe58*
- American storyteller Donna Washington makes the most of her expressive voice and face – watch her telling *Scaring Crows*: *www.youtube.com/watch?v=RFyCD-O5nbc&list=FLscW6lz3okT_y_69SsY0LGw*
- Another American storyteller, Joe Hayes, tells stories beautifully in both English and Spanish – watch him telling *A Spoon for Every Bite* in both languages, and notice how easily you can pick up another language in this way: *www.youtube.com/watch?v=5HOMPP2SzHY* and *www.youtube.com/watch?v=EBrFnwN_q7g*
- Native American storyteller Robert Greygrass tells wonderful tales from the Lakota tradition: *www.youtube.com/watch?v=TXbzcYIMi3s*
- British storyteller Jan Blake is brilliant at engaging listeners and getting them to participate actively: *www.youtube.com/watch?v=hPBjbW4L3ko*
- English storyteller Michael Dacre tells *A Spectacular Lie* – this follows in a long British tradition of satirical nonsense storytelling, and Michael is self-declared and undisputed World Champion: *www.youtube.com/watch?v=R7r369CB--c*
- Zakaria Koanda from Burkina Faso, one of my students, tells the story of *Ngolo Diara*: *www.youtube.com/watch?v=3CtUYdilRsw*

Of course, you have to remember that nothing can compare with the excitement of the 'live' storytelling experience.

Folk tales from around the world

You can find folk tales from all over the world, published in English.

Here is a new and wonderful collection:
- *www.storymuseum.org.uk/the-story-museum/chooseastory/listen*
High-quality audio recordings of brilliant storytellers telling stories, as well as simple accompanying story texts. The site is aimed at children, but is suitable for everyone.

On the same website there are also story maps to help students to retell the tales, and even a clip demonstrating how to do a story map:

- *www.storymuseum.org.uk/1001stories/detail/273/how-to-draw-a-storymap.html*

Here are more recommended web resources, where you can read huge numbers of folk tales:

- *www.pitt.edu/~dash/folktexts.html*
  A huge resource of traditional tales.
- *www.sacred-texts.com*
  Another very extensive resource.
- *www.magictails.com/creationlinks.html*
  Links to worldwide 'creation myth' resources.
- *www.chlive.org/pbeck/eastlibrary/MYTHOLOGY.htm*
  Links to traditional tales from cultures worldwide.
- *www.angelfire.com/ma3/mythology/worldtalesindex.html*
  A rich source of tales from around the world.
- *www.surlalunefairytales.com*
  The tales here come with detailed annotations.
- *www.storiestogrowby.com/choose.php*
  This website looks as if it is aimed only at children, but the content is suitable for everyone. You can find stories according to themes and categories.

And here are two highly recommended books:

- In *Favorite Folk Tales from around the World*, Jane Yolen puts together an excellent collection of world tales organised into categories. (Pantheon 1986)
- In *World Tales*, Idries Shah shows how variants of the same wonderful folk tales are told in different cultures. (The Octagon Press 1991)

Associations

- You might want to join the International Storytelling Network or at least visit the website, to find out about storytellers, events and festivals around the world:
  www.cuentacuentos.eu

- The Federation of European Storytelling (FEST) promotes storytelling and the sharing of ideas across the continent:
  www.fest-network.eu

- The Society for Storytelling website is a gateway to storytelling ideas and sources. It is a UK association, but there is also useful information for people outside the UK:
  www.sfs.org.uk
  Several other countries also have their own national storytelling associations.

In short ...

A final rhyming tale – my own reworking of a traditional Polish tale – on the next page brings my storytelling journey to a close.

- ***The Shortest Tale*** is an example of a very brief tale with actions and repetitions so it can be instantly learnt and remembered – see me telling it on YouTube. It is described as a storytelling activity in more detail here:
  www.teachingenglish.org.uk/activities/teaching-students-shortest-tale
- ***Little mouse has run, my tales are done*** is how the Brothers Grimm chose to end 'Hansel and Gretel'. It is how I often round off a performance of several stories, even with adults. It breaks the spell beautifully.

I wish you every success – as you take your next storytelling steps.

Once a poor man dug the ground,
And what he found ...
Was nothing.

Again the poor man dug the ground,
And what he found ...
Was a box.

Again the poor man dug the ground,
And what he found ...
Was a key.

With the key he opened the box,
And what he found ...
Was a mouse's tail.

And if that tail was longer ...
This tale would be longer.

Little mouse has run.

My tales are done.

From the editors

Storytelling With Our Students takes you on a highly personal journey of discovery, in the company of a teacher who is an experienced storyteller – or is David Heathfield a storyteller who is also an experienced teacher? David shows us how it is possible to be both.

- As a storyteller (or is it as a teacher?) he draws us into the world of 'world stories', of telling an unscripted story directly to our listeners – or, rather, *with* our listeners – and brings many stories from many oral cultures to vibrant life.
- As a teacher (or is it as a storyteller?) he doesn't neglect the fact that storytelling develops language skills – encouraging both speaking and listening fluency, as well as building self-confidence, increasing motivation and multiplying student interaction.

Storytelling With Our Students demonstrates the techniques for you to become successful tellers of tales yourselves – and shows how your learners will discover that they can be storytellers, too. And how your language classroom will come magically alive.

 Part A accompanies you on a journey spotlighting the history and importance of storytelling, and shows how it can be integrated into education in general and language teaching in particular – with huge rewards, not only for the teacher but also for the learners.

 **Part B** is more than just a collection of stories. David converts each one of them into an authentic activity for the classroom, highlighting specific 'telling techniques' and elaborating a series of procedures that make the most of each tale. He more than demonstrates how much there is to be gained from storytelling in language teaching.

 **Part C** presents further possibilities for those of you who enter the magical world of stories – often taking the telling of tales beyond the walls of the classroom – to show how *Storytelling With Our Students* can be just the beginning of your own journey of discovery.

Storytelling With Our Students includes stories from all around the world, and focuses on the techniques that will make all the difference as you tell them with your students.

Mike Burghall
Lindsay Clandfield

From the publisher

DELTA TEACHER DEVELOPMENT SERIES

A pioneering award-winning series of books for English Language Teachers
with professional development in mind.

**Storytelling
With Our Students**
by David Heathfield
ISBN 978-1-905085-87-3

The Autonomy Approach
by Brian Morrison and
Diego Navarro
ISBN 978-1-909783-05-8

Spotlight on Learning Styles
by Marjorie Rosenberg
ISBN 978-1-905085-71-2

The Book of Pronunciation
by Jonathan Marks and
Tim Bowen
ISBN 978-1-905085-70-5

The Company Words Keep
by Paul Davis and
Hanna Kryszewska
ISBN 978-1-905085-20-0

Digital Play
by Kyle Mawer and
Graham Stanley
ISBN 978-1-905085-55-2

Teaching Online
by Nicky Hockly with
Lindsay Clandfield
ISBN 978-1-905085-35-4

Teaching Unplugged
by Luke Meddings and
Scott Thornbury
ISBN 978-1-905085-19-4

Culture in our Classrooms
by Gill Johnson and
Mario Rinvolucri
ISBN 978-1-905085-21-7

The Developing Teacher
by Duncan Foord
ISBN 978-1-905085-22-4

Being Creative
by Chaz Pugliese
ISBN 978-1-905085-33-0

The Business English Teacher
by Debbie Barton,
Jennifer Burkart and
Caireen Sever
ISBN 978-1-905085-34-7

For details of these and future titles in the series, please contact the publisher: *E-mail* info@deltapublishing.co.uk
Or visit the DTDS website at www.deltapublishing.co.uk/titles/methodology